front porch

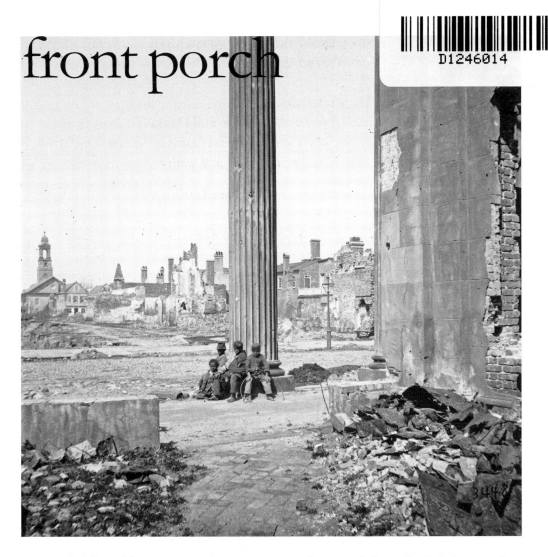

I got a childhood lesson in southern memory when my father asked if I knew what had happened in Reconstruction. I didn't, of course, but Dad left an indelible (though inaccurate) impression when he spat out the answer: "That's when white men *couldn't vote*!" It would be many years before my formal education caught up with and eventually overcame this piece of family lore, surely passed on from my father's own father, born when South Carolina was still under federal occupation. And I surely belong to the last generation of southern children to be warned against tardiness by the awful consequences of Longstreet's delay at Gettysburg.

For nearly a century, it is likely that stories like my father's taught white southerners the most powerful lessons they learned about the Civil War and Reconstruc-

above:

Here at the Civil War's Sesquicentennial, we have dedicated an issue of Southern Cultures *to southern memory, both personal and historical. Charleston, the view through the porch of the Circular Church, 150 Meeting Street, 1865, courtesy of the Collections of the Library of Congress.*

tion. Memories of victimization and outrage were the bedrock of white southern identity, so much so that the cartoon image of a superannuated Rebel shouting "Fergit, hell!" became a serio-comic icon of the War's Centennial. Black southerners had their own set of family stories and memories, radically different but much more painful. Memories have been so powerful and important in regional culture, it was no wonder that "Dixie" proclaimed that "old times there are not forgotten." So here at the War's Sesquicentennial, it is high time we dedicated an issue of *Southern Cultures* to southern memory, both personal and historical.

Our four years of remembrance are now underway. Of all the old times that Dixie was not supposed to forget, the War is the greatest, but forgetfulness now seems to be winning. The crowds at reenactments and commemorations are reportedly respectable but not huge, and there is nothing planned today that rivals the scale and intensity of the Centennial celebration of 1961–65. Among those who do remember, two dueling narratives seem to be in play, and the one I learned at home is retreating, though still putting up a fight. At the 100th anniversary of the bombardment of Fort Sumter, for example, thousands gathered on Charleston's Battery and bellowed approval with every faux shellburst. This time, the Secession Gala captured most of the headlines, but a solemn ceremony emphasizing the role of slavery in sparking the conflict won official recognition and far more participants. Today, so-called neo-Confederates proclaim loudly that the war was fought for states' rights, not slavery. Fifty years ago, the like-minded had no need for loud proclamations because most white Americans apparently agreed with them. Those five decades have made a big difference. As the Soviets used to joke about their own politically driven histories, "The present we know; the future is certain. Only the past is unpredictable."

Memory is now a favorite theme among American and European historians. As changing perspectives and conceptions have made our recovered past seem more and more unpredictable and even unknowable, some scholars have become less interested in what "really" happened and more intrigued by what people *think* happened, as well as how their memories came to be, and what they mean. An especially attractive topic is how the past is officially or publicly remembered, in monuments, holidays, reenactments, museums, and conventional wisdom. There are at least two other kinds of historical memory at work in human life, however. One kind are the biographical tales that an older generation spin about itself to the young—stories about childhood, youth, education, career choice, marriage, and maturity. These stories teach children their first lessons in how to grow up—though whether they follow them is another matter entirely. Another are the tales that elders tell children about a remoter past, the past they learned from *their* elders, that teach lessons in group identity and allegiance. What did granddaddy do in the war? What happened to our people in the old country? Did great-grandmomma tell you about slavery?

Southern cultures

Fall 2011 : Memory
Published by the
University of North Carolina Press
for the
Center for the Study of the American South
at the University of North Carolina at Chapel Hill

For the first hundred years, official, personal, and folk memories combined to tell white southerners a common tale about Civil War and Reconstruction. Stories of individual heroism, family suffering, and collective victimization flourished around firesides, school rooms, and public occasions alike, all buttressing the myth of a noble Lost Cause that brought out the best in us and deserved to prevail, but was also, somehow, a series of sad missteps that bound Americans together. We are now living through the deconstruction of that memory, without replacing it with something more gratifying. Even the glory of Emancipation cannot take its place, as that story is still told in terms of its inadequacies and disappointments, and the whole white South still struggles with its role in that drama as the national Bad Guy. Perhaps the absence of a satisfying popular memory of the Civil War has something to do with America's underwhelming response to its Sesquicentennial. For too many of us, it seems, there is nothing to mourn or to celebrate.

The authors in this issue explore a wide variety of regional and personal memories. Helen Matthews Lewis offers a straightforward remembrance of her activist career, as told to a researcher from the Southern Oral History Program. Lewis explains how she became interested in progressive social causes, where her convictions took her, and how she combined activism and scholarship. Of her marriage and her personal life, she only drops a sad hint: "it was not that bad."

Two longer essays take us straight to the heart of the Lost Cause controversy, and our shifting assessments of the Civil War era. Historian Peter Carmichael takes on the thorny question of Robert E. Lee, who was once revered as the model cavalier and Christian knight, but now faces criticism as a racist, a slaveholder, a traitor, and a bad general to boot. The result, Carmichael tells us, is a pitched battle between Lee's critics and admirers which not only reveals conflicting opinions but also conflicting ways of forming opinions in the first place. Carmichael is reluctant to take sides; he seems to have equal respect for the critics' historical methods and the defenders' longing to salvage something honorable from the War for their ancestors' memories and their own.

Sally Greene explores the lesser-known Thomas Ruffin, once praised as an outstanding antebellum judge, but now condemned as an infamous enabler of cruelty to slaves. In Lee's case and in Ruffin's, defenders denounce critics for applying modern morality outside its historical context, while challengers reply that slavery and the Confederacy had plenty of contemporary critics, so why should we listen more to one side than the other? In Lee's case, the battle lines are still sharply drawn. For Thomas Ruffin, the defense has mostly rested, and his chilling judicial decision on masters' unlimited power only survives as a classroom example of the brutality that slavery evoked from otherwise decent people. Today, Judge Ruffin's statue gathers much dust and no gazes in North Carolina's second-highest court building, banished from memory by perceived irrelevance instead of expulsion.

The next two pieces take us from the Civil War to the era of World War II.

In "'Personal in My Memory': The South in Popular Film," some of our favorite writers and critics explore the connections between the silver screen and remembering. Liberty Theatre, New Orleans, ca. 1935, photographed by Walker Evans, courtesy of the Collections of the Library of Congress.

Danny Fulks and Keith Maillard both evoke the moods of small southern towns at war, but their tales could not be more different. Fulks remembers Rattlesnake Ridge, Kentucky, as a comforting place in the 1940s, filled with human energy and foibles but swept by change as wartime industry relieved hard times, young people explored the new options brought by military service and prosperity, and old people clung to what was best about the past. Like Peter Carmichael's story about the defenders and critics of Robert E. Lee, Fulks describes the collision between tradition and modernity. In his version, the two sides are ultimately compatible and mutually supportive, producing a community that remains "southern" even as it changes.

Keith Maillard remembers a very different community. Seen through the bitter recollections of his mother and an imagined reconstruction of his father, Maillard uses empathy and unblinking insight to probe their collapsing marriage in wartime Hot Springs, Arkansas. His mother is so miserable and uprooted that she hates her surroundings, when she can bear to notice them, while his father cannot reshape his own personality to give her what she needs. It is a haunting, difficult story, reminding us that small-town life is not for everybody, especially for strangers, and carries its share of agony and suffering. As an exercise in memory, moreover, Maillard reminds us obliquely of the fragmentary and artificial nature of even the most powerful recollections, for to anyone with different ties to the community, wartime Hot Springs might appear much more like Rattlesnake Ridge than hell on earth.

On a lighter note, writers and filmmakers Godfrey Cheshire, Joe Flora, Andrew Garrison, Allan Gurganus, Randall Kenan, Elizabeth Spencer, Kenneth Turan, and Alice Walker remember for us their favorite southern movies. Any number can play. What are your favorites? Can you guess theirs? And how would you say that movies shape our memories now, when screen images can overpower family anecdotes or even personal experience in what we think we know about the past? Not one of our respondents named *Gone With the Wind*. Is that another reason why this Civil War anniversary is playing differently than the last one?

We conclude with two more slices of melancholy. Josh Eure recalls his childhood in Hertford, North Carolina, the home of famed baseball pitcher James "Catfish" Hunter. When Eure was growing up, Hertford was mad about baseball and its favorite son, but like Aileen Maillard in Hot Springs, young Josh did not fit in. He was adopted in a place where bloodlines mattered, and he wasn't much good at Little League either. Where Catfish cast radiance over everything, Josh remained in the shadows, reminding us that Hertford's timeless idyll is as streaked with ambiguity as southern memory writ large. Writer Robert Morgan drives home a similar message with three poems for "Mason-Dixon Lines." They address "memory" on the grandest scale, not familial or communal but epochal or even geologic. Morgan "remembers" the Pleistocene Era, the era of Creation, and the transformation of dust to dust. He puts our own lives in ancient perspective, smoothing out our strivings and anxieties with firm strokes from the long view. From the slaughter of Gettysburg or Cold Harbor to the sting of Josh Eure's strikeouts, human tragedies shrink toward invisibility when inscribed on an infinite calendar, but still leave sadness behind them.

Southerners today are forming and recounting new memories, from personal joys and sorrows to grand-scale events like the Civil Rights Movement or the Great Recession or the modern experiences of migration. If these memories take a regional cast, southern identity will change while remaining distinctive. If not, not. Don't forget that.

HARRY L. WATSON, *Editor*

"Truth is mighty & will eventually prevail"
Political Correctness, Neo-Confederates, and Robert E. Lee

by Peter S. Carmichael

Ways of knowing are fundamental to the interpretive battles over Confederate history broadly and over Robert E. Lee in particular. Drawing from both the modernist and Victorian perspectives can bring greater complexity to historical inquiry. Robert E. Lee, 1864, photographed by Julian Vannerson, courtesy of the Collections of the Library of Congress.

*J*efferson Davis sent Robert E. Lee an unusual note after the battle of Gettysburg. The dispatch did not contain any presidential recommendations or requests, only a clipped article from the *Charleston Mercury* criticizing Lee and his subordinates for failure in Pennsylvania. Why Davis sent this article is impossible to say, and Lee apparently was not interested in the president's motivations. The General dismissed newspaper criticism of himself as "harmless," but the *Mercury*'s condemnation of the army disturbed him. He considered the charges harmful to the cause, for his officers and soldiers were beyond reproach. Defeat, Lee insisted, was his responsibility alone. "No blame can be attached to the army for its failure to accomplish what was projected by me," he wrote, "nor should it be censured for the unreasonable expectations of the public. I am alone to blame, in perhaps expecting too much of its prowess & valour."[1]

As the press and public debated the cause and consequences of Gettysburg with nitpicking fervor, Lee assured Davis that the true story of the campaign would ultimately stand once the foamy wash of rumor and innuendo receded: "Truth is mighty & will eventually prevail." Here, Lee's theory of history reveals itself as a field of study in which objectivity, grounded in unbiased facts, leads to unvarnished truth; the reality of the past reappears in perfect clarity, full of moral and intellectual lessons for future generations to behold and absorb. Lee's understanding of history provides insight into *how* he thought and not just *what* he thought. Like so many nineteenth-century Victorians, Lee rigidly ordered the past and the present in attempts to rid himself of moral confusion, intellectual clutter, and emotional ambiguity.[2]

Lee's underlying belief in historical objectivity as the straight and narrow path to truth swayed back and forth in the unpredictable winds of war following Gettysburg, leaving him confused, depressed, and wondering if people could actually perceive the course of human events and align themselves accordingly. Although he nearly abandoned his faith in the comprehensibility of the human existence, Lee, like so many of his Confederate peers after Appomattox, sought sanctuary in the Victorian belief that the world was governed by fixed truths of right and wrong, of morality and immorality, and of purity and evil. This way of knowing, rooted deeply in the very intellectual structures of Victorianism, started to lose its dominance with the rise of modernism in the twentieth century. Yet the orientation of nineteenth-century Victorianism, in both form and content, has not disappeared entirely, even though the ideology behind slavery and hierarchy, which Lee so forcefully articulated and so unwaveringly defended, has essentially vanished.[3]

Ways of knowing are fundamental to the interpretive battles over Confederate history broadly speaking and over Robert E. Lee in particular. Americans engaged in the cultural battles over Confederate history often are caught between the Victorian belief in the knowability of the past and the modernists' rebuttal that

history is highly interpretive, constantly changing in meaning, and ultimately an expression of power and authority in society. Disagreements over Lee continue to energize historical and political debates among Americans today, and a greater appreciation of distinct cognitive styles—one rooted in Victorianism and the other in modernism—reveals how people apply their own perspectives when focusing on the past. We can, as a result, better appreciate why the wars of historical memory continue to besiege Confederate heritage and the legacy of Robert E. Lee to this day.

THE LOST CAUSE AND LEE AS A VICTORIAN HERO

The cultural influence of Victorianism continues to leave its imprint upon the ways Americans make meaning of the Civil War. Regardless of where one's sympathies lie, people who have a more Victorian disposition desire a history where sublime truths about human nobility tower above the wreckage of human existence, and where there is not the palest shadow of doubt over the future course. Victorianism serves as a simplifying cultural filter, straining out the detritus so that all that remains is a perfect gold nugget of noble truth.

While northerners might appear comparatively apathetic about the memory of the Union cause, white southerners have been tenacious in searching for moral clarity in the past. There has never been one southern white mind when it comes to the cause and consequences of the Civil War, but there have been many attempts to discover indisputable moral lessons from the years of 1861 to 1865. Shortly after Appomattox, many white southerners found intellectual and psychological comfort in the Lost Cause's depiction of a cavalier South, valiantly losing a war over states' rights, republicanism, and Christianity to the industrial might of Yankeedom. The legacy of Robert E. Lee has been central to this interpretation, while satisfying the Victorian cravings for a history where the boundary between good and evil is never blurred. When Lee died in 1870, the general was metaphorically resurrected into a Christlike figure of perfection and the embodiment of the Lost Cause as envisioned by his former comrades.

By 1900, Confederate veterans had succeeded in advancing Lee as a symbol of national reunion and reconciliation. Since then, Lee's military exploits have been widely celebrated by northerners and southerners alike, skirting difficult moral questions involving slavery and secession. Bloody battlefield victories — audaciously conceived and fearlessly executed — have and continue to capture the American imagination, fulfilling that bone-deep belief in the United States that war unleashes our most admirable qualities. Civil War buffs on both sides of the Mason-Dixon Line act out this belief when they play armchair general, getting lost in a romantic make-believe land of war, rather than confronting the tough stuff of Civil War history.

CULTURE WARS AND LEE'S HISTORICAL STANDING

Of late, however, historians have contested Lee's high standing as a general and his saintly reputation as a Christian gentleman, resulting in charges of revisionism from critics. The modernist conclusions about the general seem especially threatening to those who hold to the tenets of the Lost Cause, since such conclusions rest upon the notion that slavery was the core cause of the Civil War and the Confederate experience. This understanding has certainly encouraged new thinking about the Confederacy. Beginning in World War II and gaining traction during the Civil Rights era, it has become the dominant force of inquiry in southern history in the last thirty years.

It surprises no one today that historians ask tough questions about Lee and his fellow Confederates; what is shocking is that the rise of modernist thinking about the Virginian has infused political discourse with deep suspicion. A conspiratorial rage hijacks debate in which each side refuses to empathize with the other. Indeed, to do so is perceived to be self-destructive, a surrendering of principle, and akin to capitulation to a dangerous enemy. Without empathy, however, there can be no understanding, and the glaring absence of civility in the public discussions surrounding Lee testifies to this, underscoring a tragic turn in the United States where ideological extremism has devoured gradualism, balance, and moderation.

Many non-academics inside and outside the South deeply resent and resist any claim that slavery caused secession, that the Confederacy was devoted to human bondage, or that Lee defended the enslavement of African Americans. These same people insist that anyone who suggests that Lee fought for slavery is performing for "political correctness" theater, staged by members of the liberal academic establishment who desire nothing more than to direct a morality play in which the white South is ostracized for the nation's sins of racism. Professional historians of the modernist strain have been puzzled by this hostile response—especially since the political correctness charge suggests judgments based on contemporary moral fashions, when historians perceive their efforts to be objective attempts to contextualize Lee within the standards and mores of his era. For the most part, scholars have dueled over Lee's military record without violating the professional decorum expected of such academic debates. Not only do such discussions keep clear of contemporary politics, they also refrain from rendering moral judgments about Lee or the Confederacy. They acknowledge that slavery was a moral abomination but emphasize that the historian's task is both to take historical figures on their terms, not ours, and to understand the otherness of the past. In contrast, the non-academic Right's onslaught against academia (and the shameless politicking of a few professors in the classroom) have poisoned the public's perception of how historians teach and conduct their research.

While not every debate about Lee has disintegrated into a politically charged shouting match, many defenders of the general are lumped under the "neo-Confederate" label which in effect brands them as unabashed racists. Their views however are far more complicated and diverse. Many just want to honor their Confederate ancestors, some use Confederate heritage to advance the political cause of small government, while others associate the southern nation as a distinctly Christian one. Regardless of the perspective, they have rallied together in condemning those whom they perceive to be critics of Lee. They portray modernist historians as revisionists who promote liberal dogma by damning the Confederacy for failing to live up to twenty-first-century standards of morality. One lay critic of Lee "revisionists," for instance, recently made the impassioned pitch that any book criticizing the general is part of "the Communist dream" to eliminate "states' rights" and to create "an all powerful central government." This critic concluded: "Killing the Confederates and the Confederacy was a necessity if Americans were to learn to worship THE STATE, instead of the Lord." Although it may seem outrageous to some, this sentiment indeed is a common theme among Lee's most extreme defenders, who tend to identify with a growing right-wing populist movement that rails against a leviathan state in Washington, D.C. In turn, some critics of "neo-Confederates" tend to dismiss Lee's defenders as delusional racists

While northerners might appear comparatively apathetic about the memory of the Union cause, white southerners have been tenacious in searching for moral clarity in the past. Flag of 37th Pennsylvania Infantry, ca. 1864, courtesy of the Collections of the Library of Congress.

so taken by conspiratorial thinking and so consumed by hatred that their advocacy for small government and free-market economics is dangerously seductive to people on the margins of society. Discussions about Lee are far more than simple debates about history.[4]

HOW NEO-CONFEDERATES AND REVISIONISTS THINK

A number of writers, including Tony Horwitz, W. Fitzhugh Brundage, and David Goldfield, have brilliantly explained how both camps follow contemporary politics, not the inspiration of Clio, when exploring the past. Their work demonstrates that public controversies about the Confederacy cannot be reduced to straightforward academic questions about whether Lee was a great general, a proponent of slavery, or a model of Christian gentility. While this body of scholarship on southern memory brilliantly explains the diverse ways that people manipulate their Civil War heritage, these scholars' focus on *what* people think overlooks *how* people think. Lee's "revisionists" generally reflect an intellectual orientation influenced by modernism, with its belief in many truths and its capacity to locate the many selves that reside in each individual. The general's most strident defenders, who are mostly outside of academia, tend to attach themselves to an absolute and simplified reading of the past, fixed in meaning and time. How people think — as distinct from *what* they think — is central to understanding why some people either resist or accept the myth of Lee.[5]

To be sure, significant intellectual and political differences divide the self-proclaimed "guardians" of Lee's historical memory; unfortunately, they are often lined up under the expansive, and indiscriminate, banner of "neo-Confederate." While delineating a wide range of factions within the southern heritage movement is important to do (but rarely done), there is a similar cognitive style uniting those typically labeled neo-Confederates — and even, in some cases, those labeled revisionists. Emphasizing how people think, it is worth noting, does not diminish the importance of racial identities or other ideological beliefs. Much of the existing scholarship on the Lost Cause and Confederate heritage groups has brilliantly explored the substance of historical memories and how contemporary political realities influence the ways in which people conceptualize the past. Since Appomattox, a system of segregation, unfettered free market capitalism, and disfranchisement rested upon a view of history in which ex-Confederates were victims of a victorious North during Reconstruction, when hapless hordes were unleashed from slavery. Shifting our attention to *ways* of thinking strikes at this topic from a new angle, for it looks at the articulation process of thought as separate from, but related to, the content of ideas themselves. This adds a neglected intellectual dimension to theories of race, the politics of hate, and class alienation, all of which have been central to explaining the motivation of Confederate heritage groups.[6]

DEMONIZING THE OPPOSITION

Unquestionably, the differences between those who tenaciously defend Lee and those who won't can be deeply emotional in nature. Lee's role in the institution of slavery, for instance, is the flint that refuses to go dull, for it always draws heat, particularly among defenders who want to portray the Confederacy as a nation divorced from human bondage but devoted to states' rights. In response to a recent publication that portrayed Lee as a tough-minded slaveholder, an angry reader wrote: "This started in earnest a couple of years ago sparked by the NAACP. It all centers around the NAACP's campaign to eliminate all vestiges of the Confederacy from the face of America. They feel that as long as General Lee is held in high esteem by most Americans it presents a roadblock in achieving this goal." Conspiratorial victimization is a dominant trope among Lee's defenders, a means of claiming reverse discrimination while blaming the liberal academic opposition for using race to politicize commemorative activities. When members of heritage groups assert that they are the true purveyors of historical objectivity, that they have risen above the conformist muck of political correctness, and that through

DEFEAT IS NOT DISHONOR

When Lee died in 1870, the general was metaphorically resurrected into a Christlike figure of perfection and the embodiment of the Lost Cause as envisioned by his former comrades. Tobacco package label, ca. 1870, courtesy of the Collections of the Library of Congress.

the mist of the past they can see the world for what it actually was, they demonstrate, in effect, a Victorian way of thinking. Just as Victorians had sought perfectibility in their own lives and in their reconstructions of the past, many practitioners of Confederate heritage today want to feel good about their ancestors. This is hardly different from what most people desire when looking backward, but they appear hypocritical when insisting that they are the guardians of objective truth, while at the same time sanitizing their collective regional history.[7]

The most outspoken opponents of southern heritage groups—many of whom fall in line with the scholarly critics of Lee—have been so single-minded in debunking what they perceive as the whitewashing of Confederate history that they have not paid sufficient attention to how Lee defenders actually reach their conclusions. Too often the advocates of Confederate heritage are portrayed as unthinking thugs who are so full of race hatred, so deluded by nostalgia, and so devoted to a conservative agenda that they are incapable of independent thought. Critics of heritage groups can perhaps be forgiven for not paying attention to how their opponents think, given that elements of the neo-Confederate crowd are truly dangerous and potentially violent. However, while scores of individuals wrap themselves in the Confederate flag (when honesty should dictate the wearing of a white hood), it is too easy to write off most defenders of Lee and devotees of Confederate traditions as klansmen in disguise. Avoiding predictable condemnations of heritage groups as racists might seem impossible, especially when we encounter such

Bloody battlefield victories—audaciously conceived and fearlessly executed—have and continue to capture the American imagination, fulfilling that bone-deep belief in the United States that war unleashes our most admirable qualities. Civil War buffs act out this belief rather than confronting the tough stuff of Civil War history. Reenactment of 1862's siege of Bridgeport, Alabama, courtesy of the George F. Landegger Collection of Alabama Photographs in Carol M. Highsmith's America, Library of Congress.

irrational and angry words as those of the critic above, who has convinced himself that the NAACP wants to dethrone Lee as part of a conspiratorial insurgency against all things Confederate. Unless we get beneath the extreme emotionalism fueling contemporary memory clashes, we will be trapped in an endless cycle of conspiratorial charges and counter-charges. Shifting attention to the actual perceptions that people hold when thinking historically will promote greater understanding between academic and lay historians. We will, as a result, perceive why both camps will likely never reconcile.

The rancor of these debates now extends far beyond academic circles into the blogosphere, print media, and assorted commemorative activities, while some members of the historical establishment have fallen into this cultural gutter fight. They have defended their positions through emotionalism and easy generalizations when a more nuanced understanding of how people perceive history is badly needed. Even renowned historians make sweeping characterizations. Yale's David Blight, in a recent article in the *Chronicle of Higher Education*, observed: "The Lost

Cause tradition—as both a version of history and as a racial ideology—is certainly still very much alive in neo-Confederate organizations, on numerous Web sites, among white-supremacist groups, in staunch advocates of the Confederate battle flag, and even among some mainstream American politicians." Blight's infusing heritage into white supremacy groups under the neo-Confederate label obscures differences among legions of people who would both denounce reactionary ideology and interpret such portrayals as proof of an organized attack from "the Left." Similarly, outside the academy it is also fashionable to assume that worshipers of Lee and the Confederacy use heritage to hide hate. Social advocacy groups, including the Southern Poverty Law Center, have identified the Sons of the Confederacy and the Daughters of the Confederacy as neo-Confederate ground troops fighting for rightwing, racist organizations. While people with Aryan aspirations are sprinkled in both groups, it is impossible to quantify with any precision the number of extremists and even more difficult to determine their influence. Such a conflation allows for no distinction between unreconstructed racists and the more moderate rank-and-file members of the Sons and Daughters who are devoted to honoring their ancestors without racial animus. How can a person identify with his or her southern ancestry without being damned as a racist thug?[8]

The extreme categorizing behind this discourse has created impenetrable walls between those on both sides, who, in their separate worlds, demonize the other without having to engage in meaningful dialogue. The Confederate heritage groups, for their part, have been equally aggressive when responding to criticism of Lee. Non-academics usually describe academic critics of Lee as politically correct drones working on behalf of the liberal academic establishment. Democratic Senator James Webb of Virginia, in his book *Born Fighting: How the Scots-Irish Shaped America*, serves up an all-too-common defense of poisonous emotions and convoluted logic when he insists that the Confederate past is being condemned to Nazification: "Even the venerable Robert E. Lee has taken some vicious hits, as dishonest or misinformed advocates among political interest groups and in academia attempt to twist yesterday's America into a fantasy that might better serve the political issues of today. The greatest disservice on this count has been the attempt by these revisionist politicians and academics to defame the entire Confederate Army in a move that can only be termed the Nazification of the Confederacy."[9]

The publication of Elizabeth Pryor's recent biography of Lee, *Reading the Man*, has proved the existence of a Marxist conspiracy in the minds of some critics. "Thanks to Karl, Lincoln's Marxists/Commies/Socialists/so-called lovers of 'Democracy' have always been adept at bending those little twigs of American kids into grown-up folks who write best-selling anti-Confederate tomes," observed one angry reader. "Maintaining the present all powerful central government of today," the reader concluded, "also, depends on keeping Constitutionalists in literary bondage—by publishing and honoring only anti-South authors.

Reconditioning again and again the gullible with lies claiming the infamy of the South's great leaders is but one means of accomplishing that—for the Confederacy held the most ardent supporters of the U.S. Constitution this land has ever known. Certainly Robert E. Lee was one of them."[10]

Both sides perceive a sinister plot, barely surfacing on the political radar, hidden beneath a veil of interpretive differences, but forming an irresistible storm ready to sweep aside anyone who tries to stand against the powerful forces of conspiracy. The reverberations of such conspiratorial thinking have been felt especially in America's schools, where the creation of history standards has rung the bell for cultural pugilists to begin swinging. In Florida, to take just one example, former governor Jeb Bush signed a law in 2006 that revised teaching standards in the state's schools. Part of the legislation included the following provision: "American history shall be viewed as factual, not as constructed, shall be viewed as knowable, teachable, and testable, and shall be defined as the creation of a new nation based largely on the universal principles stated in the Declaration of Independence." Whether an individual agrees with the Florida legislature or not says a great deal about how that person approaches the past and what he or she expects to find at the end of a particular historical inquiry. The defiant stand against the historical relativism of modernism is the most striking and important feature of the bill. Moreover, this piece of legislation shows how debates over the meaning of history can become highly politicized. The tensions between Victorianism and modernism help explain why interpretive differences about Robert E. Lee are so radically at odds with each other, and how these contentious intellectual debates animate cultural wars over Confederate history.[11]

THE SCHOLARLY DEBATES

It is difficult to single out scholars who best represent the traditional and modernist followers of Lee, largely because historians tend to fly together in flocks. They follow highly coordinated historiographical patterns, wheeling one way because of new research before veering in the opposite direction in response to a recent publication. Rarely will one individual or pack of historians stray from the group and lead the way. Thus, taking aim at any one scholar of Lee might seem like a random potshot, but, as with every flock, there are birds who manage to stand outside the group, and Michael Fellman and Robert K. Krick have drawn attention to their scholarship because they explicitly articulate, unlike so many of their peers, the political and cultural implications of their interpretations. Fellman and Krick stand at the interpretive poles of the Lee debate, although they have never directly engaged each other's scholarship. Krick offers the traditionalist perspective and Fellman the modern, and from their words one can see how the threads of Victorianism and modernism sew different patterns and make for very different historical cloth.

Public controversies about the Confederacy cannot be reduced to straightforward academic questions about whether Lee was a great general, a proponent of slavery, or a model of Christian gentility. Robert E. Lee, ca. 1864, courtesy of the Collections of the Library of Congress.

Robert K. Krick, the former chief historian of Fredericksburg and Spotsylvania National Military Park, a leading preservationist of Virginia battlefields, and the author of a number of important books on the Army of Northern Virginia, is one of the most highly regarded and respected writers on Lee today. While Krick does not believe that Lee was flawless, he rarely departs from the historical gospel of Douglas Southall Freeman, whose enduring *R. E. Lee* and *Lee's Lieutenants* depict the famous Virginian as the embodiment of human perfection, both as a man and as a general. Krick's allegiance to the historical methodology of the Victorian era partially explains his tenacious defense of Freeman's principal themes as unassailable truths. He certainly has a right to endorse Freeman, especially since there are so many virtues to *R. E. Lee* and *Lee's Lieutenants*, but Krick's response to Lee's challengers is both intriguing and somewhat disturbing. He attributes the recent scholarship as part of an academic conspiracy to demolish all things Confederate. Rather than dissect the methodology and arguments of the modernists, Krick writes off Lee's critics as "bootless revisionist[s]" who have "a total lack of perspective of historical time and sense."[12]

The interpretive differences between the modernists and Lee's more traditional defenders, as Krick correctly observes, boil down to a question of perspective. But it is not, as he argues, an issue of the revisionists' lacking a historical perspective. Whereas Krick and other Victorian-oriented scholars want to recover the actions and deeds of Lee into a single grand narrative, modernist scholars believe a historical figure can be many people at once, depending on the audience and situation, making it difficult to collapse an individual's life into a single objective narrative. The methodological differences between the traditionalists and "revisionists" are further strained by the modernists' desire to roam around the mental world of their subject, which historians of Krick's persuasion typically consider nothing more than psychobabble—an abandonment of "real" evidence, the very stuff that gives history its concreteness and durability. Krick and many others of the extreme pro-Lee camp consider these imaginative interpretations as lacking empiricism and, thus, credibility.

On the other hand, Michael Fellman has advanced some of the most controversial and critical assessments of Lee deriving from modernist methodology. In the beautifully written *The Making of R. E. Lee*, Fellman's goal is to locate the "unknowable soul" of Lee. He admits that no biographer can completely capture the soul of his subject, but "that is the challenge," he writes, "and that is where imagination comes into play. Like novelists, memoirists, and historians of all stripes, biographers have fragments, sometimes lots of them, sometimes fewer, with which they must do their best to construct the richest, most complex, and at the same time most truthful, rather than true, story." Through careful research and by contextualizing the general's life within the story of his ancestry and the planter culture that produced him, Fellman reveals the many sides of Lee—the consummate flirt, the guilt-ridden Christian, a man full of lust, an unhappy husband who is sexually repressed, a devoted and loving father, a stern patriarch, a stoic Christian, and an uncontrollable warrior filled with rage. And it is these fault lines that give Lee's life not only texture but an authenticity that modernists insist cannot be found in the Lost Cause's celebration of Lee as the grand cavalier.[13]

Weighing the merits of Fellman and Krick's arguments is a distraction from the ways their methodological approaches underlie interpretive differences over Lee. It also fails to account for how ways of knowing must be considered in order to understand the nature of historical debate itself. Not all new inquiries into Lee history are from freethinking modernists, and not all of Lee's academic defenders are antiquated Victorians. The interpretive camps overlap to varying degrees, and a pure expression of Victorianism or modernism simply does not exist in any scholarly work. Intellectual tendencies, however, are discernable, and they show how the defenders and detractors of Lee operate on opposing analytical trajectories. Subordinating the content of source material is necessary at times in order

David Blight observed: "The Lost Cause tradition—as both a version of history and as a racial ideology—is certainly still very much alive in neo-Confederate organizations, on numerous Web sites, among white-supremacist groups, in staunch advocates of the Confederate battle flag, and even among some mainstream American politicians." Reenactment of 1862's siege of Bridgeport, Alabama, courtesy of the George F. Landegger Collection of Alabama Photographs in Carol M. Highsmith's America, Library of Congress.

to see how each camp interrogates and organizes sources in significantly different ways. Even though the two types of scholars dig from the same archival mines, they will most likely never come to the surface with the same interpretive findings.

Why, though, do debates over Lee become so vitriolic? Professional historians are not the victims of having their scholarly debate hijacked by frenzied masses, but many inject a conspiratorial tone into their writings, offering vague references to perverse alliances. Krick, for example, uses his review of Alan T. Nolan's provocative *Lee Considered* to characterize the "revisionist" camp as a think tank for the cause of political correctness. Academics, of course, are the main villains in his plot, and their viciousness goes unchallenged, as Krick sees it, since the political correctness juggernaut implants an irrepressible "yearning to smash idols." This desire, he concludes, "affords a limitless appeal in a smug way to the political-correctness wowsers." Who are these "political-correctness wowsers"? Krick routinely identifies Thomas Connelly, Alan Nolan, and Michael Fellman in his speeches, but this hardly constitutes a political correctness conspiracy or a substantially far-reaching intellectual movement of any kind. Nonetheless, Krick's line of reasoning, which is widely shared among the mainstream Lee traditionalists, assumes that anyone critiquing Lee's generalship is a political-correctness zealot. Of course, it is in the vagueness of the term "political correctness" that the rhetorical advantage lies.[14]

Krick's unsubstantiated charge of political correctness is hardly unique. There are many others who are far more reckless in their accusations of a left-wing academic conspiracy. Some of the most outrageous public utterances have come from Clyde Wilson, a former professor at the University of South Carolina, the author of a superb biography of Confederate general James Johnston Pettigrew, and the editor of the John C. Calhoun papers. Wilson writes in 2007, "This year is Robert E. Lee's bicentennial—the 200th anniversary of his birth. Nothing better illustrates the swift and vicious descent of Political Correctness upon American history and symbols than the shadow that has, in just the last few years, been thrown over a man regarded (rightly) for well over a century as among the greatest of Americans." He concludes, "How the times have changed, and suddenly. The official doctrine of the MSI (Mainstream Intellectuals) now condemns Lee as a traitor and oath-violator and his cause as little better than Hitler's. This interpretation rests upon either a deliberate or a vastly ignorant misinterpretation of everything important in American history. The orchestrated blackening of Lee and his cause exhibits the triumph of Marxist categories in American historiography and public discussion."[15]

When one looks beyond the words of historians like Wilson, one finds an alarming absence of evidence. Michael Fellman is the only practicing academic who has published on Lee in the last ten years who fits the "revisionist" modus operandi established by scholars like Krick and Wilson. Fellman's interpretations have a contemporary accent, especially when it comes to issues of race and sexuality. He

Democratic Senator James Webb of Virginia, in his book Born Fighting: How the Scots-Irish Shaped America, *serves up an all-too-common defense of poisonous emotions and convoluted logic when he insists that the Confederate past is being condemned to Nazification. "Even the venerable Robert E. Lee has taken some vicious hits," says Webb. The Monument to Lee in Richmond, Virginia, photographed in 1991, courtesy of the Collections of the Library of Congress.*

writes, for instance, that Lee's aggressiveness on the battlefield had a sexual function equal to the "erotic energy that had periodically forced its way up through the carefully controlled exterior the young Lee had normally shown the world in his relationships with young women." Gary W. Gallagher, George Rable, William Cooper, Steve Woodworth, Ethan Rafuse, Mark Grimsley, William "Jack" Davis, James Robertson Jr., Joseph Harsh, James McPherson, Brooks Simpson, Richard McCaslin, Steve Newton, Aaron Sheehan-Dean, Tracy Power, Joseph Glatthaar, Herman Hattaway, Daniel Sutherland, Charles Roland, Emory Thomas, Bertram Wyatt-Brown, Charles Joyner, and Carol Reardon — all part of the academy and respected authorities in their field — have offered assessments of Lee that in no way resemble the party line of the so-called "revisionist political-correctness gang." Wilson and Krick's rhetoric rests upon an imaginary group of revisionist historians working together as invisible assassins, ready to take out great Americans for the cause of political correctness.[16]

Historians like Wilson and Krick give cause and comfort to those who believe they are being persecuted for simply wanting to honor Lee or pay respect to their Confederate ancestors. Strangely, a victimization mentality takes hold among Lee's defenders, who use their persecution or way to aggressively advance their own historical and political agenda. In the spring of 2007, for instance, the Stephen Dill Lee Institute advertised a Robert E. Lee conference with the following teaser:

> 2007 marks the 200th anniversary of the birth of Robert E. Lee, one of America's most revered individuals, once esteemed in the North by his former enemies, as in the South. But opinions are changing in this era of Political Correctness. Was Lee a hero whose valour and leadership were surpassed only by his honour and humanity? Or, as some suggest today, was he a traitor whose military skill served a bad cause and prolonged an immoral rebellion against his rightful government? . . . The Symposium will cover Lee the man, his views on government and liberty, his humane attitudes toward race and slavery, Lee and the American Union, Lee as inspired commander and his relationship with the Army, Lee as a Christian gentleman, and the meaning of Lee for today.[17]

No one need dispute the S. D. Lee Institute's right to hold a conference, but the organizers should not be exempt from standards applicable to any scholarly conference in which the interpretive agenda is never set beforehand. Circling the wagons against the onslaught of the political correctness bogeyman is the rallying cry of the event, but more importantly, each line of inquiry is structured as a dichotomy demanding mutually exclusive answers. Lee was a great American *or* a cowardly traitor, a humane man *or* a sinister slaveholder, a brilliant commander *or* a reckless killer. The Victorian desire for inflexible truth, for moral lessons to appear, and for an absolute assessment of Robert E. Lee as both a man and a general permeate the conference's announcement.

Although the Lee Institute's justification for a conference is certainly troubling, we have an obligation to understand why members of this and other heritage organizations feel so threatened. We need to acknowledge that prejudices and biases exist among those who are critical of Lee devotees and Confederate heritage groups without giving credence to the ridiculous notion that a political correctness conspiracy among Marxist scholars is taking over southern history. Michael Fellman unfortunately plays into the hands of those who fear they are being hunted down by the thought police for their admiration of the Confederacy when he writes, for example: "Yet Lee's star is fading, along with the passing of segregation, and fewer Americans, even in the Deep South, still venerate Lee uncritically, although pockets of neo Confederates continue to worship him as the deity of Southern 'tradition' or 'heritage,' the code words by which they mean the old white supremacist order, based, whether consciously or not, on a belief in the natural superiority not merely of the 'white race' but of a hereditary ruling class such as the Virginia gentry." This observation too broadly categorizes those who want to honor Lee or their Confederate ancestors as racists.[18]

Careful research and contextualizing the general's life reveals the many sides of Lee—the consummate flirt, the guilt-ridden Christian, a man full of lust, an unhappy husband who is sexually repressed, a devoted and loving father, a stern patriarch, a stoic Christian, and an uncontrollable warrior filled with rage. These fault lines give Lee's life not only texture but an authenticity that modernists insist cannot be found in the Lost Cause's celebration of Lee as the grand cavalier. Robert E. Lee, ca. 1864, courtesy of the Collections of the Library of Congress.

CONCLUSION

We can bring some much-needed specificity to this intellectual and political debate by being more aware of the language employed and by questioning those who fall back on easy descriptors like "neo-Confederate" and "political correctness." Gestures on our part, however small, matter a great deal and will keep the focus on the historical subject and away from sideshow politics. Drawing from both the modernist and Victorian perspectives will also bring greater complexity to the historical inquiry into Lee. The Victorians' emphasis on history as knowable is vital if we want future generations to find relevance in studying the past. Too many academics of the modernist persuasion lose touch with reality by insisting that history is purely a construction of each succeeding generation or invented to exercise domination and power. Recognizing history as constructed cannot blind us to history as something that was experienced by real people who made real decisions and who took concrete actions. History is more than just an interpretive text or subjective words on a paper.[19]

The Victorians' insistence that history is knowable, however, encouraged intellectual arrogance through the enshrinement of universal truths. The modernists offer a proper corrective. There is no single truth but instead a historical middle ground—a "truthfulness," per Fellman—where many perceptions of the past co-exist, revealing ambiguity, contradictions, and tensions that make up the human condition. We can find the rich middle ground by returning to General Lee's tent after he read the *Charleston Mercury*. The general's own words provide valuable insights into his reaction to Gettysburg and also offer a portal into the open-ended and contradictory ways in which he tried to make sense of grand historical events, even though he was reluctant to admit that his own intellectual journey did not result in unambiguous judgments. In a July 31 dispatch, Lee told Davis that, "No blame can be attached to the army for its failure to accomplish what was projected by me, nor should it be censured for the unreasonable expectations of the public. I am alone to blame, in perhaps expecting too much of its prowess & valour."[20]

Did Lee really think he alone was to blame for Gettysburg? Or were his public confessions of guilt designed to inspire unity in the army? Postwar evidence overwhelmingly suggests that Lee was bitterly disappointed in the performance of key subordinates. In 1868, he told William Allan that "Stuart's failure to carry out his instructions *forced the battle of Gettysburg, & the imperfect, halting way in which his corps commanders* (especially Ewell) *fought the battle, gave victory, finally to the foe.*" Not only is this at odds with Lee's wartime correspondence, but Lee's 1863 claim that public criticism after Gettysburg did not affect him does not match Allan's recollections of their postwar conversations. "Gen. Lee talked feelingly of the criticism to which he had been subjected," Allan remembered, "said 'critics' talked much of that they knew little about, said he had fought honestly and earnestly to the best of his knowledge and ability for the 'Cause.'"[21]

Surprisingly, what is missing from Lee's postwar conversations is any mention of God smiting the Army of Northern Virginia at Gettysburg. In the fall of 1863 the general felt certain that God had inflicted defeat on his army for the sins of the Confederate people. "I hope will yet be able to damage our adversaries when they meet us, & that all will go right with us," Lee wrote his wife. "That it should be so, we must implore the forgiveness of God for our sins, & the continuance of His blessings. There is nothing but His almighty power that can sustain us." Lee not only worried about the South's relationship with God after Gettysburg, but he faced the practical problem of desertion gutting his army. To Jefferson Davis he admitted that large elements of the rank-and-file were badly demoralized and that only brute force would stop desertion. Almost twenty deserters were executed during the month of September alone. In his private letters, however, Lee never revealed the growing instability of his command, assuring family and friends that his army was in superb condition and excellent spirits.[22]

Lee was not a hypocrite because of the inconsistencies between his wartime correspondence and postwar remarks. Nor should these contradictions lead us to charge Lee with manipulating the historical record. The tensions among the accounts should be seen as interpretive opportunities to explore the fluid murkiness of the past where a single "real Lee" does not exist but where the many shadows of his being can be found. We cannot expect to solve the mysteries of Lee's behavior

Despite Lee's assertion after Gettysburg that "truth is mighty, & will eventually prevail," the general knew better. He knew that every student enters a bewildering maze of learning and that no one escapes with the holy grail of historical truth. Robert E. Lee, ca. 1866, courtesy of the Collections of the Library of Congress.

after Gettysburg, or anywhere else for that matter, like a basic arithmetic problem. We should embrace the fact that we will never posses a definitive answer and respect others for trying to sort out the impossible, even if we do not agree with their methods or conclusions.

Despite Lee's assertion after Gettysburg that "truth is mighty, & will eventually prevail," the general knew better. He knew that every student enters a bewildering maze of learning and that no one escapes with the holy grail of historical truth. In an 1863 letter that Lee sent to his daughter Mildred, who was struggling with her studies in Raleigh, North Carolina, we are reminded that any historical endeavor is a humbling journey in which Clio never relinquishes mastery over her student. We also need to remember that Lee wrote these inspirational words of advice when his world was filled with unspeakable violence, when he longed for the presence of his family, and when he felt a deep isolation from everyone around him in the army. If Lee could find such words of hopefulness at a time of war, then we should be able to rediscover in ourselves the joy of intellectual humility: "You say rightly, the more you learn the more you are conscious of your ignorance," Lee wrote on September 10, 1863. "Because the more you know, the more you find there is to know in this grand & beautiful world. It is only the ignorant who suppose themselves omniscient. You will find all the days of your life that there is much to learn & much to do."[23]

NOTES

This essay is based on a 2007 lecture on the historical legacy of Robert E. Lee, delivered at the Lee Chapel & Museum, Washington and Lee University, Lexington, Virginia.

1. Robert E. Lee to Jefferson Davis, July 31, 1863, in *The Wartime Papers of R. E. Lee*, ed. Clifford Dowdey and Louis H. Manarin (Boston: Little Brown, 1961), 565.

2. Robert E. Lee to Jefferson Davis, July 31, 1863, *The Wartime Papers*, 565; The secondary literature on Victorianism is vast. For a superb introduction to the subject, see Walter E. Houghton, *The Victorian Frame of Mind, 1830–1870* (New Haven: Yale University Press, 1957).

3. Elizabeth Brown Pryor, *Reading the Man: A Portrait of Robert E. Lee Through His Private Letters* (New York: Viking, 2007), 237–38; The intellectual and cultural transition from Victorianism to Modernism is expertly discussed in Daniel Joseph Singal's *The War Within: From Victorian to Modernist Thought in the South, 1919–1945* (Chapel Hill: The University of North Carolina Press, 1982).

4. Letter in possession of the author; For a superb overview of the neo-Confederate movement, see Euan Haque, Heidi Beirich, Edward H. Sebesta, *Neo-Confederacy: A Critical Introduction* (Austin: The University of Texas Press, 2010).

5. W. Fitzhugh Brundage, *The Southern Past: A Clash of Race and Memory* (Cambridge: The Belknap Press of Harvard University Press, 2005); David Goldfield, *Still Fighting the Civil War War: The American South and Southern History* (Baton Rouge: Louisiana State University, 2002); and Tony Horwitz, *Confederates in the Attic: Dispatches from the Unfinished Civil War* (New York: Pantheon Books, 1998).

6. For some of the finest work that emphasizes the role of race in southern memory construction, see David Blight, *Race and Reunion: The Civil War in American Memory* (Cambridge, MA: The Belknap Press of Harvard University Press, 2001); this insight is taken from Daniel Wickberg's "What is the History of Sensibilities? On Cultural Histories, Old and New," *The American Historical Review* 112, no. 3 (June 2007): 661–84.

7. Letter in possession of the author.

8. David Blight, "The Civil War Sesquicentennial: The Goal Should be an Enlightening Commemoration," *The Chronicle of Higher Education*, June 1, 2009, http://chronicle.com/free/v55/i38/38blight.htm (accessed June 26, 2009); for the Southern Poverty Law Center's classification of the UDC and SCV as neo Confederate organizations, see http://www.splcenter.org/intel/intelreport/article.jsp?aid=253 (accessed June 26, 2009).

9. For a good example of how the opposing sides on cultural heritage refuse to listen to each other, see http://www.oanow.com/oan/news/local/article/councilman_removes_confederate_flags_from_graves/69708/ (accessed June 26, 2009); James Webb, *Born Fighting: How the Scots-Irish Shaped America* (New York: Broadway Books, 2004), 207.

10. The American paranoid style of thinking, so closely aligned with conspiracy thought, was outlined by the great historian Richard Hofstadter, who argued that emotions associated with resentment and powerlessness deluded conservatives into seeing a world controlled by secret forces. The absence of evidence did not matter; in fact, in the minds of some it actually confirmed the presence of a sinister cabal in need of extermination. Richard Hofstadter, *The Paranoid Style in American Politics and Other Essays* (New York: Alfred A. Knopf, 1965), 3–40. An excellent summary of Hofstadter's theory of paranoia as it relates to cognition can be found in Wickberg's "What is the History of Sensibilities"; Letter in possession of author, Elizabeth Brown Pryor's *Reading the*

Man received wide acclaim, receiving both the Museum of the Confederacy Jefferson Davis Award and the acclaimed Lincoln Prize.

11. Florida House Bill 7087 (2006), 44.

12. The fact that Freeman's *R. E. Lee: A Biography*, 4 vols (New York: Scribner's, 1934–35) and his *Lee's Lieutenants: A Study in Command*, 3 vols (New York: Scribner's, 1942–44) have remained in print testifies to the enduring impact of his scholarship. For a critique of Douglas Southall Freeman's work, see Gary W. Gallagher, "Shaping Public Memory of the Civil War: Robert E. Lee, Jubal A. Early, and Douglas Southall Freeman," in Gary W. Gallagher, ed., *Lee & His Army in Confederate History* (Chapel Hill: The University of North Carolina Press, 2001), 255–82; Robert K. Krick, "Confederate Books: Five Great Ones and Two Bad Ones," in *The Smoothbore Volley that Doomed the Confederacy* (Baton Rouge: Louisiana State University Press, 2002), 233.

13. Michael Fellman, "Struggling with Robert E. Lee," in *Southern Cultures* 8, no. 3 (Fall 2002): 6.

14. A connect-the-dot conspiratorial approach that links the modernist questioning of truth to the academy and leftist politics can be found in Lynne V. Cheney, *Telling the Truth: Why Our Culture and Our Country Have Stopped Making Sense—and What We Can Do About It* (New York: Simon & Schuster, 1995); Krick, "Confederate Books," 236; Connelly was one of the first historians to explore the myth-making process of Lee. See his *The Marble Man: Robert E. Lee and His Image in American Society* (New York: Knopf, 1977).

15. On Clyde Wilson's argument that a political correctness campaign is being waged against Lee's historical legacy, see http://www.lewrockwell.com/wilson/wilson23.html (accessed June 26, 2009).

16. Michael Fellman, *The Making of Robert E. Lee* (New York: Random House, 2000), 306.

17. The program for the Stephen Dill Lee Institute can be found at http://www.lewrockwell.com/speakers/LEE_SYMPOSIUM_ANNOUNCEMENT.htm (accessed June 26, 2009).

18. Fellman, *The Making of Robert E. Lee*, 306; Even in popular culture, Confederate heritage groups serve as easy targets for ridicule. In a 2007 monologue, comedian Jay Leno suggested that Don Imus, after being fired for racist remarks aired on the radio, planned to raise funds for his favorite charity, the Sons of Confederate Veterans. The Sons' leaders denounced Leno's comments for implying the group was racist. While some might consider Leno's joke as harmless fun, it is understandable why these popular misperceptions might make the people behind the Confederate heritage movement feel besieged, causing them to become insulated, defensive, and in the end, vulnerable to reactionary politics. Tony Horwitz, in his brilliant *Confederates in the Attic* discovered during his odyssey across the South an incredible diversity in heritage groups. Ed Ayers makes a similar argument in "What we talk about when we talk about the South," in *What Caused the Civil War?: Reflections on the South and Southern History* (New York: W. W. Norton & Company, 2005), 37–63.

19. For an encouraging example of opening a debate with the so-called neo-Confederate side, see William L. Ramsay, "Horowitz, Genovese, and the Varieties of Culture War: Comments on the Continuing Unpleasantness in Idaho," at History News Network, http://hnn.us/articles/23113.html (accessed June 26, 2009).

20. Robert E. Lee to Jefferson Davis, July 31, 1863, in *Wartime Papers*, 564.

21. William Allan, "Memoranda of Conversations with General Robert E. Lee," February 15, 1868, in Gary W. Gallagher, ed., *Lee the Soldier* (Lincoln: University of Nebraska Press, 1996), 14, 15.

22. Robert E. Lee to Mary Anna Lee, July 15, 1863, in *Wartime Papers*, 551.

23. Robert E. Lee to Mildred Lee, September 10, 1863, in *Wartime Papers*, 597–98.

"Personal in My Memory"
The South in Popular Film

**by some of our favorite writers and filmmakers
with an introduction by Godfrey Cheshire**

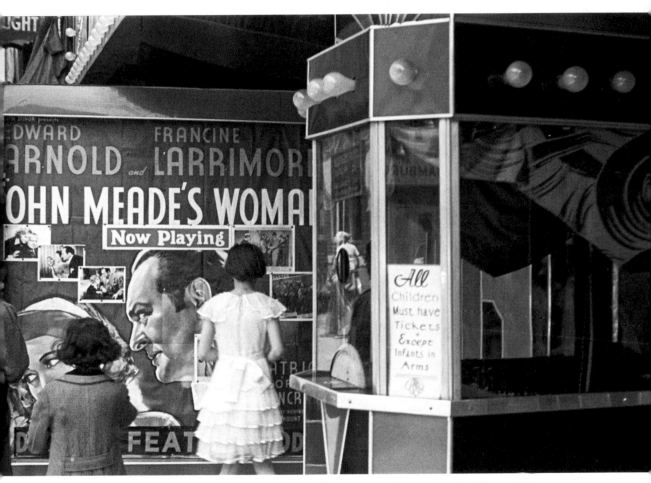

"We have two imaginary kingdoms. One, 'the South,' exists primarily in song, oral traditions and folkways, native art and literature. The other, 'Hollywood,' creates mass-produced audiovisual entertainments for American and world audiences, and develops its own mythology." Moviegoers at a D.C. theater, 1937, photographed by John Vachon, courtesy of the Collections of the Library of Congress.

If you're ever inclined to doubt the importance of the South to American movies—or vice versa—consider that David Wark Griffith's *The Birth of a Nation* (1915), the foundation stone upon which the whole edifice of the American movie industry is built, and itself still perhaps (depending on whose figures you believe) the most successful film ever made, is a radically atavistic epic purporting to explain the entire sweep of southern history. A key document of southern cinematic literature, it is set mainly in the South, and was directed, brilliantly, by one native southerner (from the writings of another, novelist-racialist Thomas Dixon Jr.), but was filmed in a place whose fame, at the time, was yet to come: Hollywood, California.

Thereafter, we have two imaginary kingdoms. One, "the South," exists primarily in song, oral traditions and folkways, native art and literature. The other, "Hollywood," creates mass-produced audiovisual entertainments for American and world audiences, and develops its own mythology. Occasionally, sometimes frequently, the two kingdoms interact, but their relations are uneasy because they are not equals. Hollywood, the colonizer, is happy to exploit the tales, myths, culture, and sometimes the great talents (see: W. Faulkner, screenwriter) of the South, but invariably imposes its own language and concerns on the southern raw material, feeling no particular obligation to "get it right." For its part, the South nervously contemplates the resulting distortions of its self-image(s), though it will swoon (along with the rest of the world) at the appearance of a romantic, Hollywoodized South, such as that in David O. Selznick's 1939 production of *Gone With the Wind* (another film with a claim to be history's highest-grosser).

Among moviegoers, there are as many Souths as there are individual sensibilities to discern them in the theater's darkness. Nevertheless, certain patterns become evident. For some viewers, as the essays below indicate, the films that impress derive from valued southern literary sources; here, Hollywood's translators have presumably not distorted those sources too greatly. Two writers, on the other hand, find wonderment in films that come from pre-existing southern sources, a pop song and a best-selling novel, precisely because of the way cinema's magic *has* transformed them; here, Hollywood is an unwitting agent of personal revelation. For one northern-born critic, there's a late-dawning realization of how the movies confuse the real South and its fictional apparitions; he confesses that two Hollywood films have long made him avoid the region. And as if to prove that any "southern film" is ultimately personal, one writer names a quintessential New York-set film simply because it offers a few glimpses of Florida, a place that many southerners don't even consider part of the South.

Finally, there's an essay that points us toward the startling notion that, while most cinematic visions of the South from *The Birth of a Nation* till now have come

Alice Walker on Cold Mountain: *"I was probably the last person on earth to see the movie* Cold Mountain, *but I finally saw it and valued it: it cured me of my inability to feel compassion for the soldiers who fought on the Confederate side in the Civil War."*

to us filtered through the aesthetic/industrial lenses of Hollywood, they don't have to be. From the time they began appearing the 1970s, the documentaries of North Carolina-born Ross McElwee have posited and exemplified an idea of film as an equivalent of southern literature: personal, idiomatic, made from a native's point of view, untouched by Hollywood motives or money. If many of the films discussed here belong to a past where movies in general were the property of Hollywood, it could be that McElwee's work points toward a future in which some visions of the South can genuinely be called southern films.

ALICE WALKER ON *COLD MOUNTAIN*

I was probably the last person on earth to see the movie *Cold Mountain*, but I finally saw it and valued it for three reasons: it cured me of my inability to feel compassion for the soldiers who fought on the Confederate side in the Civil War; it made one young soldier come vulnerably alive, showing how important it was in those days for a family during winter to have a hog to kill and eat (they were like my own family); and it showed a wise woman living in the woods with her goats and how she killed one of them while its head was in her lap and she was stroking and lovingly murmuring to it. She then cooked some of the meat for the wounded soldier to eat. That depiction, of how killing an animal might be done, is one I appreciate because it reminds humans that though we must eat other living beings to live, we do not have to withdraw our affection when it is most needed and abandon our sustainers in their moment of transition.

Renowned author, essayist, and poet Alice Walker is the author, most recently, of a collection of poems, Hard Times Require Furious Dancing *(2010), and the memoir,* The Chicken Chronicles *(2011). This remembrance is adapted from a post on her blog, "Alice Walker's Garden," www.alicewalkersgarden.com, reprinted with permission.*

ALLAN GURGANUS ON *SHERMAN'S MARCH*

Hollywood finds the South uncontainable in ninety minutes. All trees get draped with plastic Spanish moss. All actors' rustic accents make our teeth hurt. (The worst twang ever? I nominate Jane Fonda's in *Hurry, Sundown*. Praline-batter producing sugar-shock.)

I prefer my bourbon made in Kentucky, then served straight-up. Ross McElwee's *Sherman's March* (1986) is a home-brewed masterpiece, time capsule-worthy. Its southern accents all ring genuine. Both the American Civil War and this film might be characterized: "a point of view in rebellion against itself."

When the true history of documentary film is written, McElwee's centrality will come clear. Director Michael Moore has said, "I did not go to film school. I went to Ross McElwee films and stayed all day."

Gone With the Wind was shot in California by Californians and starred a lovely Englishwoman. *Sherman's March* is made in the South by an upper-middle-class Carolinian observing flawed similar Carolinians. That makes it so thoroughly Carolinian it first gets scary then hilarious. McElwee is not James Agee—dressed in rags while spying on the rural poor—moved at his Shakespearean largesse over their ringworm. No, McElwee knows: white people rich enough, if filmed at home by relatives, will get on camera and say exactly what they think. Terrifying. You have to have parents like these to truly understand.

McElwee's film manages to out-Gothicize any stranger's comic horror film about the South. *Sherman's March* is not mere autobiography; it confesses past the point of crazed bravery. Personal faults are addressed in successive depth-charge questions we all recognize: *Where is Love? Even if I found it, would it ever be enough to compensate for sure-thing Death? Wouldn't I be safer marrying outside my religion, my region? Should I change my name?*

In 1985, McElwee won a grant to chronicle General Sherman's victory-lap march seaward. That campaign had intended to dispirit—via fire—Confederate civilians. The present film begins like any B-minus burned-map Ken Burns epic. But McElwee's mock-somber voiceover soon admits losing interest in this very project. Why? His girlfriend just dumped him! She, presumably a clueless Yankee, has damaged the civilian morale of this North Carolina doctor's son. So, instead of marching into Reconstruction, we are rerouted to Rehabilitation. The new march, exceedingly dangerous, hopes to find this boy a Southern Ms. Right. We get a road movie. But, because it's about men seeking women, it remains a war movie.

Allan Gurganus on Sherman's March: *"McElwee's pitiless take on his own self-pity puts him in company with Walker Percy's hilarious and spooky* Moviegoer." *Walker Percy (light trousers), entering the Varsity Theater in Chapel Hill, North Carolina, courtesy of the North Carolina Collection, the University of North Carolina Library at Chapel Hill.*

Few people film their own first dates. Surely there's a direct ratio between the camera's presence and the probability of your getting a second date. We encounter one young man, as horny as forlorn, as funny as Woody Allen (back when Woody thought "funny" was almost enough). *Sherman's March* becomes an ambush of blind dates. Some are engineered by friends of the filmmaker's parents, and at family cookouts! We witness, with ever more guilty pleasure, real-life fix-ups even worse than our own very worst. Girls most like the filmmaker—in terms of privilege, education, Scotch-Irish freckles—all turn out to be "born-agains" even crazier than he. We have entered the purgatorial Confederacy. This is not the Deep South of the low-thread-count Klan. No, we're locked into the gated communities of golf-crazed Presbyterians. Such ghettos prove more deranged than even General Grant once feared.

McElwee's pitiless take on his own self-pity puts him in company with Walker Percy's hilarious and spooky *Moviegoer*. We come to love this romantic pilgrim's progress. The young man imagines himself ready for Universal Adventure and a Southern Woman, not necessarily in that order.

We feel the loneliness of a boy behind the lens as serial women flirt him into deeper insignificance. Yes, Scarlett, the South is still a Matriarchy. And it takes a passive Protestant man with a camera this witty to fully admit it.

Allan Gurganus is the author of Oldest Living Confederate Widow Tells All, The Practical Heart, *and other fiction. He wrote and narrated the BBC's "A House Divided: Poetry of the American Civil War." Gurganus's novel-in-progress is "The Erotic History of a Southern Baptist Church."*

RANDALL KENAN ON *ODE TO BILLIE JOE*

And Papa said to Mama as he passed around the blackeyed peas,
"Well, Billie Joe never had a lick of sense, pass the biscuits, please"
—Bobbie Gentry, "Ode to Billie Joe"

This is Romeo and Juliet set in post–World War II rural Mississippi. Romeo is played by Robby Benson, 1976's version of the Jonas Brothers all wrapped up in one; Juliet being a doe-like Glynnis O'Connor, whom the camera loves. The picture: *Ode to Billie Joe*, being Max Baer Jr.'s second movie. (He being the son of the heavyweight champion boxer Max Baer, and once Jethro Bodine of *The Beverly HillBillies* fame in his youth.) Based on the hit 1967 song by songstress Bobbie Gentry. Baer's first big hit, the first of a short run of memorable movies about the Dirty South, tinged with erotica and nostalgia, a far cry from the Clampetts, yet not quite Walker Evans and William Faulkner either . . . unless you count his notorious *Sanctuary* . . .

I saw it at a small theater in Wallace, North Carolina, when I was but thirteen. It is a painfully simple story: small-town boy courts and sparks a small-town girl; they fall in love; boy falls, by wicked external influence, into a night of debauchery (an act only hinted at on camera); he cannot forgive himself, and, like some Protestant American Martyr, ends his life, leaving his beloved to ponder and spin and wonder. ("Today Billy Joe MacAllister jumped off the Tallahatchie Bridge.")

It was the first movie I remember haunting me and actually causing a mild depression. Melancholy. I was too young to have a sense of surety (What did Billie Joe McAllister do to cause himself so much pain?); my notions were inchoate, and too vague even for a premonition. I probably knew the word "homosexual," but its meaning was but an urge in my pants and far from any reality. Yet what I am certain of now is the sense of dread, the Signs in the Sky, the warnings and omens, the prefiguration of doom: Beware all ye who enter here. There be Dragons there, y'all!

But what hateful Dragon could smite the lovely Robby Benton? (I sometimes jokingly say Robby Benton made me gay.) Shame on that damn Dragon! The penultimate scene in the woods: over-written and over-acted, and embarrassingly powerful exactly for that reason; so true to the adolescent spirit, lacking in all taste or any sense of proportion; so in love with its own melodramatic knowledge of being alive and of having feelings—the scene where a cast-away Billie Joe, all sweaty and mottled with dirt and peat, comes upon his lady love, in a glade, after having foraged for days alone in the wood: here he confesses, at the same time, of his profound lust for her, and of his now-corruption, obviously beyond Christian redemption, all this before running off to jump his young life away into the Tallahatchie River. To this day that humid scene still shatters my heart, despite Max Baer's clumsy but well-meaning hand. I felt naked when I watched it, revealed, and feel naked even now when I see it.

Randall Kenan is the author of several works, including Let the Dead Bury Their Dead and Other Stories *and* The Fire This Time, *and the editor of* The Cross of Redemption: The Uncollected Writings of James Baldwin, *for which he wrote the introduction. He is an associate professor of English and Comparative Literature at the University of North Carolina at Chapel Hill.*

KENNETH TURAN ON *THEY WON'T FORGET* AND *I WAS A FUGITIVE FROM A CHAIN GANG*

When I was a boy growing up in Brooklyn, New York, my only exposure to the South was through the old Hollywood movies I watched on television, and two of the ones I saw made an especially powerful impression: *They Won't Forget*, starring Claude Raines and loosely based on 1913's Leo Frank case, and the self-explanatory *I Was A Fugitive From A Chain Gang*. Both were socially conscious films from the 1930s, both were directed by Mervyn LeRoy, both were based loosely on true stories, and both scared the heck out of me, leaving me with the strong feeling that the South was not exactly a place that was friendly to outsiders. Many years have passed since then, but when I consider why I've never spent extended time in the Deep South, not even for a visit, I wonder how much my childhood memories of those movies have held me back.

Kenneth Turan is film critic for the Los Angeles Times *and National Public Radio's "Morning Edition." His latest book is* Free For All: Joe Papp, the Public and the Greatest Theater Story Ever Told.

JOE FLORA ON *SWEET BIRD OF YOUTH*

When I was in the third grade in Saginaw, Michigan, the Daniel Theatre first opened its doors a mere three blocks from my house. The double-feature was its forte, and during my elementary school years, I was a patron usually twice a week, and sometimes more. In those years, I encountered the films and stars of the thirties and forties—the great and the mediocre. Among them I found my first images of the South. *Gone With the Wind* gave me my first imaginative encounter with the Civil War, and whatever her faults, Scarlett O'Hara captured me. I began to learn about serious film.

A love of stories, whether on the page or on the screen, made an English major the inevitable choice for me in college, and in time, I would come not only to teach the plays of Tennessee Williams but to study the film adaptations as well. In

Joe Flora on Sweet Bird of Youth*: "A love of stories, whether on the page or on the screen, made an English major the inevitable choice for me in college, and in time, I would come not only to teach the plays of Tennessee Williams [right, with Andy Warhol in 1967] but to study the film adaptations as well." Photograph by James Kavallines, courtesy of the* New York World-Telegram *and the* Sun Newspaper *Photograph Collection at the Library of Congress.*

1962, the year that I moved to North Carolina and my immersion into southern life began, Williams's *Sweet Bird of Youth* hit the nation's screens. Almost as if heralding the turbulence of the Civil Rights Movement just ahead, the film accented the racial drama that Williams had encoded in his play about fleeting youth, tortured love, and artistic struggle. For the first time, Williams confronted the themes of lynching and racial victimization that he had previously kept distant.

Unusual for Williams, *Sweet Bird of Youth* has a real villain. He's Boss Finley (Ed Begley). The Boss exemplifies southern politics at its worst. Draping himself with the flag—the Confederate flag—he campaigns in the rhetoric of Christian religion. He casts himself as a Christ-figure, called to deliver his people and protect their purity. *His* people are white people, and he images southern womanhood through his daughter Heavenly (Shirley Knight). Heavenly is beautiful, blond, and always dressed in white. The "Dixie" played at the film's political rally is spirited; the silence comes when we hear the solo "Rock of Ages." The rock of Finley's creed is, it becomes clear, white supremacy. Any unrest in the community he blames on "outside agitators." The Finley Youth Club (read Ku Klux Klan) works behind the scenes to deal with "agitators."

We find no black women characters in the film. There are two very handsome black men—one young, one elderly. The young man works as a bellhop at the hotel where the prodigal Chance Wayne (Paul Newman) returns in hopes of reclaiming his great love, Heavenly. The bellhop is obviously intelligent and full of promise, but he knows his place. If he continues on that path, he may find the security of the trusted black butler who works for Boss Finley. Both roles are minor, but telling. Looking closely, we realize that the film is about the black man—virile and threatening to the Southern Lady. In Boss Finley's eyes, Chance is that threat, and he must be dealt with just as sexually threatening black men are dealt with. At the end of the film, the "Klan" punishes Chance for his "defilement" of Heavenly. We see Chance held down on the hood of an automobile, his legs outspread. Finley breaks his nose, scarring the beauty that had made Chance so attractive to women. In the play, Chance is actually castrated—the sacrificial lamb on that Easter Sunday. Williams and the filmmaker have been, in the words of Toni Morrison, "playing in the dark"; Chance has become the black man.

Sweet Bird of Youth would have been too sexually explicit for the 1940s, but had it been made and had I been allowed to see it, much of it would have gone over my head. I'd have been pulling for Chance and Heavenly, of course, happy for the Hollywood ending that sent them off to start a new life together. I'd have taken huge pleasure when Aunt Nonnie gets the feel-good last line. "You can go to hell!" she tells Boss Finley. But I'd have missed the meaning of all the Confederate flags and the playing of "Dixie" and unaware of the messages these symbols sent African Americans. Now, however, I see that the film was reaching far deeper than even viewers of 1962 could have seen. *Sweet Bird of Youth* was ahead of its time in many ways—and it has lessons still for our time.

Joe Flora is professor emeritus of English at the University of North Carolina at Chapel Hill.

ANDREW GARRISON ON *MIDNIGHT COWBOY*

In *Midnight Cowboy*, Ratso Rizzo (Dustin Hoffman), an Italian-American New Yorker, longs for the paradise of Florida, my home state. His friend Joe Buck (Jon Voight) helps him get there before he dies. The closing music, "Everybody's Talking at Me," is a plaintive and evocative song written by the great Fred Neil of Coconut Grove, Florida. Of *course* people in New York want to live in Florida. My Italian American mother and Ukrainian/German American father moved to Florida in the postwar boom to get out of New York and Philadelphia. I always felt lucky to have been born in—and to be living in—that lush, subtropical paradise.

When they finally make it on the Greyhound to South Florida, Joe Buck gets out to get Rizzo . . . some water? He meets the first smiling face he's seen in a long while, a young waitress from a donut shop. And when Joe gets back on the bus, Rizzo has died. Like most of the audience, tears welled up in my eyes. At fifteen I knew it was all right to cry, but I also knew I really shouldn't.

I loved the story, and I shared Rizzo's and Fred Neil's desire to be in Florida. But what really made the movie special for me was glimpsing a little of my hometown, Hollywood, Florida, from the bus window. That donut shop, a Dunkin' Donuts off of Hollywood Blvd., was my and my best friend's favorite hangout. We'd go there for coffee and a donut after a night of homework or a day spent snorkeling. In the movie, the bus passes over a bridge so small you wouldn't notice it if you didn't know the geography already. That's Sheridan Street, where another friend, Johnny, and I traversed that very bridge talking about God and Life and Death. I was thrilled to see my private localities in so public a way. It was as if my inner life was visible in the movies, legitimized, even celebrated.

Independent filmmaker Andrew Garrison teaches production at the University of Texas. His current project, Trash Dance, *is a feature documentary about the collaboration between a choreographer and employees of the City of Austin's Department of Solid Waste Services.*

ELIZABETH SPENCER ON *INTRUDER IN THE DUST* AND *THE REIVERS*

Two movies based on Faulkner novels I remember especially. One was *Intruder in the Dust*, which was filmed on location in Oxford, Mississippi, while I was teaching at Ole Miss. Some of us were delighted to follow the film crew around at night in the woods around Oxford and to later see in the film how some of our friends appeared as extras in crowd scenes. The part of Chuck was ably played by a boy actor, Claude Jarman, and Miss Habersham (Elizabeth Patterson) was well done also. But the part of Uncle Gavin (David Brian), which should have furnished a meaty southern role as a small-town philosophic lawyer, was not memorable. We must look to Gregory Peck in *To Kill a Mockingbird* for a perfect portrayal of a similar character. For the role of Lucas Beauchamp, an actor from Puerto Rico, Juano Hernandez, came to Oxford. In that segregated time, he was required to live in the black section. However, the maid of a friend of mine reported that they liked him fine and that they took him to church.

Another Faulkner novel, *The Reivers*, was also personal in my memory as it was shot in Carrollton, Mississippi, my own hometown. I lived in Montreal at that time, but I heard a lot about it from my mother's letters. Steve McQueen, playing Boon Hogganbeck, was a big presence in town throughout the filming. He romanced all the elderly ladies, who were charmed. My mother wrote me that "Mabel and Leila are crazy about Steve McQueen, but to me he's not a patch on Cary Grant."

Elizabeth Spencer on Intruder in the Dust*: "The part of Uncle Gavin (David Brian), which should have furnished a meaty southern role as a small town philosophic lawyer, was not memorable. We must look to Gregory Peck in* To Kill a Mockingbird *for a perfect portrayal of a similar character." From* To Kill a Mockingbird, *a Universal release, copyright 1962, courtesy of the Museum of Modern Art Film Stills Archive.*

The movie was shot in Carrollton rather than Oxford because, while Oxford had changed over the years since the time the book was set (early twentieth century), Carrollton had never bothered to change at all. In Montreal when the film was released, I could see homes and streets, the courthouse square, and familiar faces from my childhood. The movie itself seemed to me a successful realization of Faulkner at his comic, affectionate best. The scene of the horse race, when the winning horse is urged on the scent of sardines, hit a high mark in the ridiculous.

Elizabeth Spencer's writing has received numerous awards, including the Award of Merit from the American Academy of Arts and Letters, the PEN/Malamud Award for Short Fiction, and the Lifetime Achievement Award from The Mississippi Institute of Arts and Letters. Her most recent book, The Southern Woman: Selected Fiction *(2001), has recently been released as a Modern Library trade paperback, and a documentary film about her life and work,* Landscapes of the Heart: The Elizabeth Spencer Story, *is pending release.*

Editor's Note: In memory of scholar and friend Bernard Timberg, who first proposed this feature and helped guide it to publication.

No Sweat
Memories of Southern Appalachia

by Danny Fulks

"They called the president 'Ruz-velt' or 'Rosy'; but after Pearl Harbor, with boys going off to war, Rattlesnake Ridge folks did let up on him a little bit." The USS California *ablaze, Pearl Harbor, Hawaii, 1942, courtesy of the Collections of the Library of Congress.*

n the late 1930s, folks living on Rattlesnake Ridge, Kentucky, saw signs of trouble. Way off. Men and women talked about news from over the waters; an uneasiness showed in their faces. I heard it from hungover veterans of the First World War who picked up stories from meetings of the American Legion and Veterans of Foreign Wars clubs in Catlettsburg, Kentucky, an old Ohio River town with a southern aura; a town where locals recollected past days when packet boats from New Orleans used to put in after a slog up the Mississippi to the Ohio and on up North. Getting off the ridge once a week, men, women, kids, and hired hands crowded into old Model A Fords, shuffled over to Simms Grocery and Dry Goods in Flatwoods, Kentucky, to trade eggs and chickens for sugar and lard, look over new Home Comfort stoves. A worker in the store demonstrated ways to use white oleomargarine, mix it with a yellow powder so it looked like butter. Few were interested. They'd been making pure butter from raw milk all their lives; it was bad enough to fool with ration stamps for sugar and gasoline. Gossip about recent arrests by the constable, new candidates up for county commissioner, and the sweetness of Stone Mountain watermelons passed among the shoppers.

Cooney Simms, the grocer, had a big Philco floor-model radio with push buttons and short wave. Neighbors gathered around when Joe Lewis was fighting. And wasn't he always, this good giant who whipped Adolph Hitler's man Max Schmeling? Static wasn't too bad; one could hear Franklin Roosevelt's fireside chats if they didn't come on the same time as the Grand Ole Opry. Gabriel Heatter broadcast out of New York City on Sundays, signing on with, "Ah, but there's good news tonight." Good news? Maybe a laugh on Jack Benny or "Fibber McGee and Molly." If another war was coming, men wondered if the price of tobacco would stay up—still hating Roosevelt, even though they got more cash money with fewer pounds than they used to. Republican, Protestant, conservative—however, they took to electric power and price supports on tobacco. Refrigerators, washers, lights, radios became common. Tractors replaced horses. Small farmers who didn't have a truck hired someone to carry their chickens to market or to haul a bulling cow up the road to a neighbor well-off enough to keep a bull for stud. They called the president "Ruz-velt" or "Rosy"; but after Pearl Harbor, with boys going off to war, Rattlesnake Ridge folks did let up on him a little bit. Funny songs like "You're a Sap, Mister Jap" drew smiles as they came in clear by radio on cold winter nights; something to hum while they milked instead of Jimmie Davis's "You Are My Sunshine."

Elton Britt sang: *God gave me the right to be a free American/And for that precious right I'd gladly die/There's a Star-Spangled Banner waving somewhere/That is where I want to live when I die*. Jukeboxes, radios, and record players spread the words and melodies. Young men from the ridges and bottoms—drunk at Shorty's beer joint in Catlettsburg—heard the song over and over, groused out the next morning, and joined

"Uncle Sam's draft notices came by Rural Free Delivery to men from ages twenty to thirty." The author's older brother, Atlee Fulks (here, in 1945 on an M4 Sherman tank near Berlin), earned four bronze battle stars. Photograph courtesy of the author.

the Army. Might as well. Uncle Sam's draft notices came by Rural Free Delivery to men from ages twenty to thirty. Forget mama, papa, girls, basketball, putting up hay, and dreaming of good $300 used Fords and Chevys, sharp roadsters with rumble seats, suicide doors, spare tire covers with BURGER BEER written on them.

Holy Roller preachers rode high, played up ghastly fears of kids dying far from home. They were bound to get them saved and sanctified in case they came back in a coffin. Men gave up on having a young wife, a house full of kids, crops of tobacco on hillside flats, a few acres of corn on bottomland, and trapping muskrats in steel traps set on the banks of the Big Sandy River. The old folks felt fear and separation. The young picked up romantic visions from magazines and movies of travel to lands unknown, where people passed the nights away with cold beer, poker games, piano bars, and the musky aromas of strange perfumes. And days rumbling along roads in places like Lawton, Oklahoma, in Jeeps and big 4x4 Army trucks whose air brakes gave off loud whooshes at stoplights.

The Andrews Sisters came through: *Don't go walkin' down lovers' lane / With any-one else but me / Anyone else but me / Anyone else but me / No! No! No! . . . 'til I come march-ing home*. Rattlesnake Ridge boys weren't big on jitterbugging, ill at ease as they were at square dances, fiddle contests, and on the rosin-sprinkled dance floors in roadhouses along Kentucky State Route 23. But they heard the bouncing melo-dies, the earthy lyrics, the jazz beat of big-city horns. Used to sad hymns, songs about dead babies, gold streets in Heaven, they were ready for new tunes. Girls promised to wait for dear boyfriends until the War was over—true bluein' 'em all the way. Couples rode along two-lane roads on Saturday nights loved up in rattle-trap cars as gears ground from the stick shifts. The radio played: *There'll be smoke on the water / On the land and on the sea / When our Army and Navy overtake the enemy*. Pretty good fun, but bigger adventures lay ahead. Red, white, and blue posters in post offices and filling stations and on high-school bulletin boards proclaimed: WIN THE WAR. Still, old men in the summer of 1942 traipsed along ditch banks, long hillside flats of watermelon vines, their gnarled faces and hands, dark bib over-alls, long-sleeved gray shirts with exposed patches of brown dirt, as one with iron weeds; slow-moving images blended into redbrush and encroaching honeysuckle vines. And the old women cooked three meals a day in the summer heat on wood-burning stoves, pulled weeds from gardens between meals, swatted flies, and read the Bible. Men respected the Sabbath, sat in the shade and smoked after church and dinner.

Boys went through lines in county court houses, copies of *Greetings from Uncle Sam* stuffed in their shirt pockets. Word was, if you wanted a good spot, a better deal, get to town fast; those with pregnant girlfriends had already packed for Fort Bliss. Forlorn at first, girls became resigned, showed off boyfriends' class rings for 1942, made to fit with a couple of inches of yarn wrapped around them. Owners of big bottomland farms along the Big Sandy used political pull to get deferments for their sons and farmhands. But few were left out. Boys with Packard convert-ibles parked under the shade of giant oaks, along with those who grubbed brush in new ground for a dollar-a-day, headed off to Fort Leonard Wood, Fort Sill, and the godforsaken Parris Island, South Carolina, where sand fleas bit the year around. *Semper Fi*.

Boys on the move away from Rattlesnake Ridge, with paperwork stamped and crimped, were sustained by roll-your-own Bugler cigarettes and plugs of Star chewing tobacco on their first ride in Pullman railroad cars. One way. They and kids from all over the East Coast sang the same songs, drank beer, played cards, sat side by side on bar stools, shared smokes on Friday nights after long days of harsh cussing and humiliation by drill sergeants. City boys puked in dark alleys, swore to beat the hell out of peckerwoods from the Ridge after being talked into

"Furloughs were hard to get, but most boys made it back a few times, showed off their uniforms, took a few days of the old home life. Out at night, they ran into old friends and younger boys ready to get in." The author, age eleven, wears older brother Atlee's Army jacket and plays soldier in front of the family's northern Appalachian vernacular frame house, 1944; photograph courtesy of the author.

trying chews of homemade twist tobacco. Black boys left lives of severe poverty, too—but in different train cars, different jobs hidden away in the Quartermaster Corps, where they loaded trucks and ships, drove gas tanker trucks, served in the Military Police. Back on the Ridge, the happy days Roosevelt promised finally came.

God was on our side. In Protestant churches, mothers with bobbed hair asked for special prayers for boys over the waters, cried as they went through the box of civilian clothes the mail brought a few days after their boys left. Music came in from radio station WWL, New Orleans, with studios in the Roosevelt Hotel, brought new tunes like "Coming In on a Wing and a Prayer" and "Praise the Lord and Pass the Ammunition." Kids on school buses rolled along gravel roads, broke into harmonies on Spike Jones's "Der Fuehrer's Face" and Carson Robinson's tune: *We're going to have to slap, that dirty little Jap / And uncle Sam's the guy who can do it / We'll skin the streak of yellow from this sneaky little fellow . . ."* And the junior high schools' mixed choruses practiced: *Over hill, over dale / We have hit the dusty trail / As those caissons go rolling along.* Teenagers with cars and a few bucks took in movies in

"Soldiers told stories of dodging rocket bombs sent over by the Germans, whiskey in forty-ounce jugs, and the wild streets around Piccadilly Circus in London; girls who liked to make out standing up, offered a good time for a pack of Pall Malls. Back at Parris Island new recruits came in daily." Members of a Marine balloon barrage unit in training at Parris Island, South Carolina, 1942, courtesy of the Collections of the Library of Congress.

Huntington, West Virginia, at the elaborate Keith-Albee Theatre: *Hitler's Children, Flying Tigers, Thirty-Seconds Over Tokyo.*

Strange names became familiar. Weird caricatures of Heinrich Himmler, Hermann Goering, Von Ribbentrop, Tojo, Hitler, and Mussolini appeared in newspapers and magazines, their names spoken daily on the radio. Used to names like Sheets, Scott, McGuire, Cox, Watson, Carter—the very sounds of foreign names evoked hatred and fear. But a message of hope came up from Nashville: Cowboy Copas and his band played a gig at Flatwoods High School dressed in matching satin stage gear, made everyone proud as they sang: *She's my Filipino baby/She's my treasure and my pet, loving pet/Her teeth are bright an' pearly/And her hair is black as jet.* You see, Filipinos hated the Japanese, too. Copas sold songbooks after the show, signed autographs. And if a boy wrote back from Germany that he was bringing a fräulein home with him, no sweat on that; made wives as good as local girls—well known they didn't sass their men, did what they were told, like the Bible said.

Men too old for the war and those classified 4-F rolled in money from jobs in war plants turning out nitroglycerine, steel, shell casings, and railroad cars. Young women went to town, got jobs, liked them; a paycheck, friends, a sense of belonging—more fun than the old folks who went to bed with the chickens and believed one swallow of whiskey was as bad as a gallon. With their boyfriends off to war, they left their mothers with tasks like putting up beans for winter, took to smoking, greeted strangers in uniforms as they passed through towns, served homemade cookies, danced, listened to the sounds of bebop and boogie woogie. Scared at first by dudes in zoot suits and heavy watch chains, young women loosened up, knocked back whiskey sours, gin fizzes, and pulled on red-tipped cigarettes. Neon signs blinked through the nights in the new world beyond Rattle-snake Ridge where a coolness they never dreamed of existed, lives and times they'd only seen in movies. The world could be on fire, but in Louisville all was copacetic. And the fever simmered on.

Soldiers sent back pictures and letters, told about bacon and eggs on Sunday mornings in the mess hall, cold beer on Saturday nights, pool in the Day Room at the end of the month when money was short. They told of skills they had learned, stuff they could use when they got out: maintenance work on airplanes was bound to be the coming thing: removing engine cowling, greasing joints in wheel wells, fixing gas leaks, testing hydraulic lines, cleaning flaps and trim-tabs. They worked for that second stripe to earn five dollars more a month. Rumors about German mechanics with calibrated eyeballs who could set spark plugs without using a feeler gauge passed among crews on the flightline.

Furloughs were hard to get, but most boys made it back a few times, showed off their uniforms, took a few days of the old home life. Out at night, they ran into old friends and younger boys ready to get in. High school juniors and seniors were taken by tattoos of naked girls and martini glasses; tickled about tales of Italians, Jews, Mexicans; learned every American Indian in the Army was called "Chief." And what about those British girls who couldn't wait to give up dart games and warm ale in village pubs to come to the United States? Soldiers told stories of dodging rocket bombs sent over by the Germans, whiskey in forty-ounce jugs, and the wild streets around Piccadilly Circus in London; girls who liked to make out standing up, offered a good time for a pack of Pall Malls.

Back at Parris Island new recruits came in daily, soon to chant as their heads bounced up and down in awkward formations of close order drill, Marine style:

The second lieutenants will win the war, parley voo,
The second lieutenants will win the war, parley voo,
The second lieutenants will win the war, so what the hell are we fighting for,
Hinky Dinky Parley Voo

"Anyone here from Kentucky?" the drill instructor yelled.

"Yo," said the redheaded boy from Olive Hill.

"Get off your ass and pick up the goddamned cigarette butts."

"Yes, sir!"

Folks back home were the ones who had it rough. Gas, sugar, and meat were rationed. Roosevelt wanted scrap iron; Eleanor urged everyone to plant Victory Gardens. Gardens? People on Rattlesnake Ridge had lived out of gardens for a hundred years. Drummers called on mothers with kids in the service, pushed patriotic items like satin window banners with a blue star for each family member gone to war. They offered up prayers that the family would never need one with a gold star, but left a business card just in case. Radio announcers peddled kitsch like REMEMBER PEARL HARBOR lapel pins for women. A fake jewel replaced the word "pearl." Months came and went, home life in wartime became routine, men

"Hot movie stars, fast cars, short skirts, French kissing, modern motels, four-lane blacktops, easy money, ducktail haircuts, and school sock hops baffled preachers." Kentuckians listen to a mid-century itinerant preacher, courtesy of the Collections of the Library of Congress.

carried in coal, built fires, sorted tobacco into grades of tips, bright leaf, red leaf, lugs, and packed baskets for the Maysville, Kentucky, auction house.

During the Christmas season of 1944, houses along Rattlesnake Ridge sat in peace under a winter moon. Inside, mothers and children decorated pine trees brought in from the woods. Grandmas made pies and oyster dressing. Near the city of Monschau, Germany, Junior Belville, from Greenup, Kentucky, lay dead in a snowbank, frozen stiff. His body was recovered by an Army graves registration crew when they cleaned up after the Battle of the Bulge, Hitler's last stand, a feeble attempt to break back into Belgium. The day Junior's momma got the message her son had been killed, she ran screaming down the road in an awful terror. They cancelled school for the funeral a few weeks later. Old men from the VFW came out. One played "Taps" on a bugle, another gave Junior's mother a folded American flag. She kept it on a pillow in her parlor the rest of her life. And she treasured a letter from her son she received after the funeral. Junior told about being asleep under blankets and a layer of snow near a forest. He felt someone kicking at his shoes, yelling, "Wake up, goddamn it!" "Are we moving up?" asked Junior. "Hell no, we're moving back," the lieutenant said. GIs on a short-lived retreat.

Anthony Carter came home the following January with both legs amputated. Uncle Sam gave him a 100 percent disability check for life and a new Chevrolet sedan with hand controls for the brake and clutch. In a few weeks the Russians took Berlin, the Americans came in from the West, and the war in Europe was over. The Japanese, leery of the Russians coming their way, in despair after Truman dropped the Big One, got smart, met with Dugout Doug MacArthur on the deck of the USS *Missouri* in the Pacific, signed off on papers to end the war on that side of the world. The rest of the men came back a few at a time as they had left, went into Catlettsburg, signed up for rocking-chair money. No longer firmly attached to place, they married, moved on up North where the steel mills in Youngstown, Canton, and Detroit ran around the clock, turning out big iron for cars and refrigerators. Back on Rattlesnake Ridge and along the Big Sandy, lonely moms and dads waited again for their children to come back on weekends to visit, smell summer rains, trudge up hills and knolls to old graveyards on Decoration Day, sit in on back-porch guitar pulls. Sunday afternoons they loaded their cars with their moms' covered dishes, vegetables, twists of homemade tobacco, and headed back North. Guitar pickers formed bluegrass bands, played gigs in back-street beer joints where country folks hung out, worked out guilt in storefront Pentecostal churches; women cooked up pinto beans and peach cobblers, even though they had money for White Castle burgers and beef filets. Trips back home became fewer as their kids got older, found lives of their own; couldn't miss soccer games on the grass fields in the Akron suburbs.

A few veterans from the ridges and hollows went off to college on the G.I. Bill, became teachers and lawyers. Farmers left behind slowed down with old age, waited for a big company to buy their land for coal or a shopping center; sat in the shade of sugar trees as summers came and went, drew their old-age pensions, and lived a nineteenth-century life to the end. Merle Travis sang his hit song "Divorce Me C.O.D.," a favorite in roadhouses, a look at the coming years of money, mobility, and anonymous lives. Veterans back in civilian life learned to tie Windsor knots, wear Palm Beach suits. Cheap money from GI loans put families who'd never seen an inside toilet into good houses. Hot movie stars, fast cars, short skirts, French kissing, modern motels, four-lane blacktops, easy money, ducktail haircuts, and school sock hops baffled preachers. But their fight against worldly pleasures on Rattlesnake Ridge never let up.

Mountain Feminist

Helen Matthews Lewis, Appalachian Studies,
and the Long Women's Movement

FROM AN INTERVIEW BY JESSICA WILKERSON

COMPILED AND INTRODUCED BY JESSICA WILKERSON

AND DAVID P. CLINE

This 1966 photograph of Helen Matthews Lewis outside of a mine entrance embodies her life; it is a portrait of the scholar as coal miner, the worker as scholar, and the academic as activist. Photograph courtesy of Helen Matthews Lewis.

A 1966 photograph of the Appalachian historian and activist Helen Matthews Lewis captures much about a woman who has been studying, writing about, and fighting for the people of Appalachia for three-quarters of a century. In the photo, Lewis sits outside of a mine entrance, hair emerging beneath a hard hat, with a big smile and coal-smeared cheeks.[1] It is the portrait of the scholar as coal miner, the worker as scholar, the academic as activist. The image of Lewis in the garb of a coal miner—hard hat, head lamp, and rolled up sleeves—anticipates the 1970s movement of Appalachian women into the male-dominated coal industry following Title VII legislation, while also recalling Lewis's own history as a trailblazer for women in the academy.

Helen Lewis has long been a towering figure in Appalachian Studies, designing the first academic programs and developing an interpretation of Appalachia as an "internal colony" of the United States, a model that influenced a generation of Appalachian scholars and activists.[2] She describes herself as part of the "long movement for women's rights." Her experiences as a child in rural Georgia, her education at a progressive women's college, and her tireless efforts working for justice in Appalachia and the South are emblematic of how a generation of southern women activists who came of age in the 1940s confronted racial, gender, and class discrimination in their native region.

While Lewis's scholarship has been profoundly influential, her personal story is less known. As she recounts it, early encounters with a range of social movement activities informed her work. Lewis's activist career began with the YWCA as an undergraduate at the Georgia State College for Women in the 1940s, where she participated in interracial organizing. As she entered graduate school and began teaching anthropology and sociology in the 1950s, she navigated an academic system that discriminated against her because she was a woman and the wife of an academic. After she left academia, she became an important ally and supporter of grassroots women's activism in Appalachia. Although women's equality was not always at the forefront of her activism, Lewis's struggle for gender equality and her awareness of how it relates to class and race equality weave throughout her narrative.

She was born in Jackson County, Georgia, in 1924. Her mother was a home-maker and dental assistant, and her father was a rural mail carrier who had high hopes for his two daughters, Helen and JoAnn. Despite her loving and secure family, Lewis witnessed the injustice of the Jim Crow racial caste system. She tells a story of meeting a black schoolteacher who was on her father's mail route and whom her father held in high regard. The teacher wrote her name on a card in beautiful calligraphy, and she speaks of cherishing that card and keeping it for years. When she was seven or eight years old, the same man came to her home to see her father. "Mr. Rakestraw is at the door," young Helen announced to her mother, who was quilting with other white women. "The women laughed because you weren't supposed to call a black man 'Mister,'" Lewis explained. "I was so shamed by that . . . As a child, to be laughed at is a terrible thing."[3]

When Lewis was ten years old, she and her family moved to Forsyth County, Georgia, where whites had forced nearly all black people out of the county in 1912. Her father, who did not agree with the violent treatment of African Americans, used his position as a mail carrier to warn those who did come into town that Forsyth County was not a safe place for them. Lewis says her father provided a foundation of fairness and caring that later influenced her interracial activism during her college years and her work long afterward. Yet, the story about Mr. Rakestraw captures the social contradictions that she faced as a young woman: her mother allowed her to play with African American children—and behaved kindly toward African Americans—but did not question local customs; her father actively tried to protect African Americans from dangerous encounters in the county.

After graduating high school, Lewis headed to Bessie Tift College, a small Baptist women's school. There she had her first "conversion experience"—the moment when she began to think more critically about race relations in the South. Clarence Jordan, the white preacher who founded Koinonia Farm as an intentionally interracial, religious community in Americus, Georgia, exposed her to a liberal Protestant Social Gospel message: justice and equality should be realized in the here and now. After completing a year at Bessie Tift and taking a year off to work, Lewis entered Georgia State College for Women (GSCW). In the early 1940s, the YWCA sponsored Lewis and a friend as they attended an interracial program in which students worked together on industrial projects at Hartford Theological Seminary in Connecticut. There she lived in integrated cooperative housing with students from across the country. Not only did Lewis have opportunities to travel and meet people from different regions, the Campus Y exposed her to some of the most progressive public figures of her day, including the Presbyterian minister Charles Jones, a leader in the progressive Fellowship of Southern Churchmen, and Lucy Randolph Mason, an organizer for the Congress of Industrial Organizations (CIO). While these people and experiences helped her envision a more just society, she also came face-to-face with the repressive politics of Georgia segregationists. She relates these stories here.

In 1946, Georgia became the first state to allow eighteen-year-olds to vote, and Lewis joined the GSCW League of Women Voters and led a campaign to register young voters. After graduation in 1946, she went to graduate school at Duke University, and there she met Judd Lewis, whom she would soon marry. He wanted to attend the University of Virginia for his PhD in philosophy, so she went with him and completed her MA in sociology in 1949. Her thesis, "The Woman Movement and the Negro Movement: Parallel Struggles for Rights," draws historical

Lewis's mother allowed her to play with African American children—and behaved kindly toward African Americans—but did not question local customs; her father actively tried to protect African Americans from dangerous encounters in the county. Photograph courtesy of Helen Matthews Lewis (here) with her sister Jo Ann (to her right) and parents.

comparisons between the U.S. suffragist movement and the early stirrings of the African American Civil Rights struggle.

In 1955 Helen and Judd both took jobs at the newly opened Clinch Valley College in Wise, Virginia. Marriage policies at the college restricted wives of male faculty from holding full-time positions; thus, Helen taught sociology part-time and worked part-time as a librarian. Not until the late 1960s did she receive a full-time faculty position in sociology and anthropology at Clinch Valley. In 1970, she received her PhD in sociology from the University of Kentucky, and her dissertation, "Occupational Roles and Family Roles: A Study of Coal-Mining Families in Southern Appalachia," again showed her ongoing exploration of identity, in this case regional and gender identities among coal field communities.

While the Civil Rights Movement was taking off in much of the South in the 1960s, Lewis lived and worked in rural, largely white communities tackling the oppressive policies of the coal companies that dominated politics in the coalfields of Appalachia. Yet, her activism in Appalachia was not isolated from the insurgent Civil Rights Movement; her work demonstrated similar concerns about equality,

economic justice, authenticity, identity, and democratic government as the organizers for freedom in the Deep South. Indeed, Lewis's academic work forged a
connection between her region and the Civil Rights Movement; the Appalachian
Studies program she developed at Clinch Valley in the late 1960s influenced a cadre
of activists, including grassroots leaders and white Civil Rights activists who migrated to the mountains to build alliances with rural whites. Together, they forged
a progressive movement in Appalachia in the late 1960s and 1970s.

Lewis's proposal for the Appalachian Studies program reveals her approach to
life in Appalachia and to her academic study of the region: "The education process
must provide a true understanding of the history and exploitation of the area and
a commitment to creative change. Education must be directed to changing the
system by educating change agents and the resources of the colleges must be used
constructively to attack real problems in the area . . ."[4] Her philosophy of education embodies a commitment to creative change, and it was likely influenced by
the citizenship schools that spread throughout African American communities in
the South.

After a long struggle with university gender policies and a series of confronta-
tions with powerful coal corporations in the local government and college, Lewis
left formal academia in 1976 and continued her commitment to democratic education as a staff member at the Highlander Research and Education Center. This
adult education center in New Market, Tennessee, fosters grassroots and social-
justice organizing, and sociologist Aldon Morris characterized it as one of the
Civil Rights "movement halfway houses" that inspired and nurtured participants.
While at Highlander, Lewis showed special interest in local women's involvement
in community activism and was keenly aware of how poverty and sexism inter-
twine in Appalachian communities. Drawing on her experience with women's co-
operatives and economic education programs, she co-edited the handbook "Picking Up the Pieces: Women In and Out of Work in the Rural South."[5] Her two
most recent books, *It Comes From the People: Community Development and Local Theology*
(co-authored with Mary Ann Hinsdale and S. Maxine Waller) and *Mountain Sisters:
From Convent to Community in Appalachia* (co-authored with Monica Appleby) evidence the pervasive Social Gospel discourse, although with a distinct Appalachian
flavor that still permeates much of the progressive social activity in the region.

Lewis is currently working on a book manuscript about the progressive activities of the Campus Y in the South. She herself is also the subject of a forthcoming
academic work, *Helen Matthews Lewis: Living Social Justice in Appalachia* (University
of Kentucky Press), a collection of articles, interviews, and abstracts from 1942 to
the present, honoring the career and vision of this pioneering spirit.

She sat down for this interview last year as part of the Southern Oral History
Program's "Women's Movement Project," a component of the SOHP's research on

the "Long Civil Rights Movement." What follows is Helen Matthews Lewis, in her own words.

GROWING UP IN CUMMING, GEORGIA

When I moved to Forsyth County [at the age of ten, I] discovered that this was a county with no African Americans in the whole county. Some ten or fifteen years before, [local whites] had accused this black [man] of raping a woman—one of those episodes—and they ran every black out of the county, took over their farms and whatever they had. I was told stories about how they hung blacks around the courthouse. I know they at least lynched the guy that they were accusing of this, and I don't know how many others. Some people maybe have done some research on it, but the stories were told. I could just see bodies hanging all around the courthouse, in my mind as to what happened. So it was . . . horror. And then blacks coming in through the town on trucks to deliver stuff to the stores were afraid to get out of the truck. They would hide in the back. I found this to be just horrifying, but somehow I never quite got it connected with doing anything about it or thinking about it in that way.

My father came home from the mail route one day, and he said he saw this old black man bicycling through town and he was on his way to Gainesville. And he said, "I'm worried he's got to go through Chestatee." The young Chestatee boys were the ones that started the riot—the rowdy boys of Chestatee. They threw all the blacks out. He said, "He'll never make it to Gainesville." So he gets in his car. "I'm going to go find him." He goes and picks him up and takes him to Gainesville and comes back. So, there was that little bit of episode.

It was a real backwoods little town at that time. It was our first move to what I call "the mountains." Now, Appalachia legally includes Jackson County, but we were more like hill country. The hillbillies lived up here, you know, more in the Blue Ridge area. When we got to Cumming there was a lot more country or mountain culture there, even though it's just forty miles from Atlanta. In my classes [in the fifth grade] very few people had even been to Atlanta, and [our teachers] took us on a field trip. We'd go to the cyclorama and the zoo and see the city.

So it was quite a real country town. I mean, there were not even sidewalks. One year they did sidewalks and all the kids in town got skates—and it was not safe for anybody to walk on the sidewalks because we were all skating. We even skated in the middle of the highway, all the way up toward Dawsonville. Dawsonville was the moonshine capital of Georgia at that time, and all of these people, who became race car drivers, were running liquor every night down the only paved highway in north Georgia at that time, the road between Atlanta and Dahlonega, which came through Cumming. And the state police would be chasing these rum

Lewis's activism in Appalachia was not isolated from the insurgent Civil Rights Movement. Indeed, Lewis's academic work forged a connection between her region and the Civil Rights Movement. Harlem demonstrators in support of the Selma's Civil Rights marchers, 1965, photographed by Stanley Wolfson, courtesy of the New York World-Telegram *and the* Sun Newspaper *Photograph Collection at the Library of Congress.*

runners every night, so that was our sport, to say, "Oh, there goes Parker C.," or "There goes—." We knew them all by name, the drivers of the cars.

WHO IS THE GOOD SAMARITAN?: HEARING CLARENCE JORDAN SPEAK AT BESSIE TIFT COLLEGE'S CHAPEL AND HAVING A "CONVERSION EXPERIENCE"

When I was in high school—those experiences in Forsyth County—there was a sense of horror, but I had not connected it with religion or anything.

Chapel was required [at Bessie Tift]. I'm sitting in chapel, paying no attention, and this young man [Clarence Jordan], who had just graduated from Southern Seminary, told how he had bought this farm in south Georgia and was going to have an integrated communal farm with blacks and whites working together. [Jordan] had re-written all the gospels, the *Cotton Patch Gospel*, which he had written as if they were talking about today. He told the story of the Good Samaritan, in which the Good Samaritan is a black man, and he tells it in a southern dialect, almost, is the way he talked. He says, here's this preacher running down the road in his Model A Ford, getting ready to go to church and singing "Brighten the Corner Where You Are"—he acts it out—and he says, "Oh, look at that poor fellow over there. Well, I don't have time; I've got to get there and open up the church and see how many people I can get saved today." And the Good Samaritan ends up being this old black man in a wagon who treats [cares for] the guy, and then at the end it's like, *who is the Good Samaritan?*

It was like a flash of light or something. I call it a conversion experience. I said, "My God, that's what religion's all about. That's what it's all about." And so it was from then on that I became an activist.

1942–1946: THE GEORGIA STATE COLLEGE FOR WOMEN CAMPUS YWCA AND INTERRACIAL ORGANIZING

After a year back at home I went to Georgia State College for Women, and there I became involved both with the Baptist Student Union and with the YWCA. The student YWCA was at that time pushing for integration—that was the mission of the student Y—and they would take you to integrated meetings and integrated conferences. They would have these conferences at Paine College, the black college. So I got involved in going to integrated meetings. I spent a weekend at Atlanta University, living in a dormitory with black students, and had some really interesting experiences, changing all my views. I didn't have the real problem that other students did whose parents were real racists, because my father, even though he was not an activist, was this gentle, caring person, and they had no objections to my doing these things.

One summer another student and I did "Students-in-Industry" [a YWCA program to expose students to wage work, politics, and social life in urban centers] at Hartford Theological Seminary. We rode a Greyhound bus all the way from Atlanta to Hartford, Connecticut; it took three days to do it in those days. This was of course during the war and there were lots of problems with transportation and a lot of servicemen on the bus, and two nights you were on the bus. We all had to find jobs, and it was a great group. It was about eighteen of us. There was one black student and one Japanese student, American Japanese, but he'd been in one of the concentration camps until that summer and then been released to go to MIT. We lived in this co-op house together and cooked together. The black student was

Helen Matthews Lewis: "I'm part of the long women's rights movement, I'd say. I remember when I was writing my thesis. I wanted to live in the 1830s and to have been at Seneca Falls. I really identified with all of those early abolitionist women." Abolitionist and author Harriet Beecher Stowe, 1880, courtesy of the Collections of the Library of Congress.

from Harvard and came from a very upper-class family who did not want him to participate, because there were going to be these two young girls from the South there, who they thought would mistreat their son. As it turned out he became one of our very best friends, and he and the Japanese guy and my friend and I hung out together the whole time and did all sorts of things together.

The Y at that time was a very important part of the whole college. The woman who was the Y secretary was on the staff, and they were given the job of doing the religious emphasis week — all the speakers for chapel — so they brought in all of these radical speakers, mostly from labor unions, and ministers who were really preaching social gospel, which was pretty radical. Then people like Clarence Jordan came, and he would do workshops. Frank McAllister from the cio would come. Lucy Randolph Mason, who was this wonderful woman organizer, labor organizer — she would come speak. Everybody was part of the Y. Now later the schools got rid of the ywca because it was so radical. It was really radicalizing students. Not everybody attended these things, but I just happened to be one of the ones that did. And the ywca secretary had an apartment, a sort of open place, where we would go for breakfast and pancakes and discussion. And every speaker we had—afterwards, we would have meetings with them and ask questions and sit around on the floor.

BEING CHARGED WITH DISORDERLY CONDUCT AFTER ORGANIZING AND ATTENDING AN INTERRACIAL MEETING IN 1948

In Atlanta, on the Emory campus, I take a job for the summer working with the YWCA. I am in the office, and we have this group of seminarians who come down to do service learning jobs. They're staying out at the black college, because there's one black student in the group. The Fellowship of Reconciliation [an international pacifist organization founded in 1914] was sponsoring them, and they asked the Y if we would have a little reception for them. I said, okay, good, and I'll invite all these YWCA girls who are here for the summer. Some of them have just graduated—and they've got jobs—and one of them was working with the Girl Scouts and stuff. We had this reception for this group, and another black couple comes with them. And the police raid us and arrest us for disorderly conduct and disturbing the peace.

They didn't take us to jail. They pulled us out individually, and the policeman said to me, "What would your daddy think if he saw you dancing with a nigger?" We had been doing this little play party game, something like the Virginia reel [a folk dance] or something like that. Then they gave us all a ticket, and then we were to go to court. Well, the day we were to go to court the Klan marched against us, and [segregationist Georgia governor] Herman Talmadge was running this big newspaper, the *Statesman*, at that time. He jumped on the case, so we were getting too much publicity. Finally, we had a lawyer, James Mackay from Emory, and he got the disturbance of the peace, disorderly conduct, dismissed. Oh, it made the front pages of the *Atlanta Constitution* and the *Atlanta Journal* and listed everybody's name and where they lived. Girls lost their housing. Some of them lost their jobs. Their families went into hysterics because [the newspapers] said "arrested at mixed dance."

That was another experience which was important in my life.

THE DECISION TO MARRY, FEMINISM, AND ATTENDING THE UNIVERSITY OF VIRGINIA

[Getting married] was considered the thing to do.

I'm working in the governor's office. [My boyfriend Judd Lewis was] at Emory, and he would visit every weekend. Of course, my family liked him. My sister thought it was great. All my girlfriends thought it was wonderful, and they

"There were really, really strong women in the '30s. There was Eleanor Roosevelt. There was Frances Perkins [U.S. Secretary of Labor]; there were role models. There were women that were very, very strong union organizers. Lucy Randolph Mason." Eleanor Roosevelt, talking with a machinist during her goodwill tour of Great Britain, 1942, photographed by Toni Frissell, courtesy of the Collections of the Library of Congress.

planned what they would be [in our wedding]. And he does this really awful thing at a gathering, a party: he comes up with this ring and proposes—I mean makes a real definite proposal. He'd been talking about it, and I just kept saying, "no, no, no." I was just caught. I was really caught, and being a nice southern girl you don't talk back that much, you know. I mean, now I think, *Why did I do that?*

Anyway, it was not bad. It was okay. But he wanted to go to the University of Virginia; that was the philosophy department. I did not want to go to the University of Virginia, [but] we had worked up this idea of this perfect partnership, you know. We would have this partnership marriage, and we would find a place where we could both teach. And so I applied to go to the University of Virginia. Floyd Nelson House, who had come out of the Chicago School, was there, and he wrote back and said, "Really, you ought to go some other place. We don't have that good a program. But if you want to come we'll give you a Stokes Fellowship, and you will work on something that will be related to race relations."

I thought, "Okay, that doesn't sound too bad."

He said, "We don't give a PhD. We just give a master's," so maybe we could work out something and "you could go somewhere else."

He was not real encouraging. I mean, he said we'd love to have you, *but*.

So anyway, I end up in that department, and [House] was quite a good social theorist. Also, I had this Stokes Fellowship, and I was to do something related to race. I had read [Gunnar Myrdal's *An American Dilemma: The Negro Problem and Modern Democracy*]. It had just come out, and in the back was a little appendix that talked about the comparison between women and blacks or slavery and how similar it was. So I decided that that was what I would do my thesis on: the women's movement. It's called "The Woman Movement and the Negro Movement: Parallel Struggles for Rights." It was published [in 1949] in a little Phelps Stokes Fellowship paper, a booklet.

In some sense this was in-between the suffragist movement [and the second-wave feminist movement], and a lot of my teachers at GSCW came out of that first [campaign for] women to vote, a lot of women who were old suffragettes. They pushed us really hard on the importance of a women's college—that women can do anything. If you'd been at the University of Georgia, they'd say, you'd be secretary; here, you can be president. There, you'd be a cheerleader; here, you play the sport. I mean, they pushed us to be feminists.

I was already an outspoken student at that point, but not quite as strong in terms of marriage. It still was the thing you did—and it was before the Pill, so if your hormones are raging you got to get married. There wasn't any such thing as trial marriages or living with somebody or anything like that. Anyway, we had a good time at the University of Virginia. It was not that bad.

THE WOMEN'S MOVEMENT

I'm part of the long women's rights movement, I'd say. I remember when I was writing my thesis. I wanted to live in the 1830s and to have been at Seneca Falls. I really identified with all of those early abolitionist women. I just felt like that was where I should have been—that's who I was—but I was in the 1940s and '50s by then. So when the new women's movement began, I fell right in. I think that I was one of those hanger-on-ers that kept something going, at least in myself, during the period when there wasn't much of a movement. But I don't think it ever completely disappeared. You can talk about the first wave, second wave,

"While we're up there [in New York City], the Young Lords had taken over this church, and they were like the Black Panthers, and they said, 'Well, you know we probably will be busted by the police pretty soon and probably killed. Anybody that tries to do any change gets killed.' And of course there was Martin Luther King, the Kennedys — all that had happened by then." Robert Kennedy, then New York's senator, and Donald F. Benjamin, of the Central Brooklyn Coordinating Council, surrounded by children, 1966, photographed by Dick DeMarsico, courtesy of the New York World-Telegram *and the* Sun Newspaper *Photograph Collection at the Library of Congress.*

but [the Y and probably other women's organizations] kept the movement going, maybe even some missionary societies. I don't know. I know [you wouldn't think] some of those literary clubs were progressive at all, but I bet you some of those tea parties had also led to some solidarity of women. They were like women's support groups, if nothing else. And those 4-H Clubs and home demonstration clubs. My mother was part of a home demonstration club back in the '20s and '30s, and she even went to a conference at the University of Georgia and left my sister and me just with my father. That was really weird that she would do that, you know.

But I think those home demonstration clubs were largely related [to a women's movement]. Unfortunately, they got taken over by the electric power companies that were selling electric stoves and modernizing cooking and selling stuff. I think we need to really re-look at what was happening to women in that period, between what you would call the real suffrage movement and the vote, and when Betty Friedan and those people came forth. I think that we missed giving credit to some of those things that were happening. The YWCA was very deliberately working to promote women's empowerment and things, but these others—probably, that wasn't their mission. But I think they were filling a role that we've not understood fully.

There were really, really strong women in the '30s. There was Eleanor Roosevelt. There was Frances Perkins [U.S. Secretary of Labor, 1933–1945]; there were role models. There were women that were very, very strong union organizers. Lucy Randolph Mason. There were all sorts of people at that period of time, and there was this group of women who helped organize and get Highlander going and who were union organizers.

But there was this real macho thing, and I guess your style of confrontation was—I don't know if you'd call it more gentle or more subversive. I mean, you learned how to get around it without putting up your dukes. You catered to certain things, but then you just did what needed to be done—and maybe you had to pretend somebody else thought it up. Women have done that all their lives. If you judge the degree of authority that women [had to assume] against [their actual authority]—where you didn't have that much in terms of legal position—[then] you worked in other ways. You could still make a difference.

THE TREATMENT OF WOMEN FACULTY DURING THE 1950S AND '60S, AND A SUMMER IN BERKELEY

I was hired both to teach sociology and be librarian [at Clinch Valley College], a double job, but they would not hire me full-time. I was part-time temporary. I was not covered by any of the perks, because I was married—and the University of Virginia at that time would not employ both a husband and a wife. What they did was exploit the wives by having them work but not be "full-time employees," although I was working full-time. I don't know how they were able to do that. But anyway I started pushing. I fought with the University of Virginia for fifteen years.

So I decided to go back [to school], and I applied and got a National Science Foundation grant to go for the summer to Berkeley. I get on a train in West Virginia and ride all the way to California for the summer for this particular workshop for people who taught anthropology but didn't have degrees in anthropology. It was to be a degree program where you could get your PhD, but you had to go three summers and go back and do certain things within your class, like how you teach anthropology and what it was all about. Anyway, I had this great summer in Berkeley the year before the free-speech movement, and every movement, every problem, issue, was being talked about and had booths all over the campus. It was the most exciting, thrilling experience to be in Berkeley at that particular time.

I come back all ready to really do this, and the librarian is gone from the college. I had been the librarian for four years; then they had finally gotten a librarian, and I was just teaching. I come back to teach anthropology, and I have to be librarian again because their librarian is gone—and they promise me that they're going to give me a real job. Well, they didn't.

It wasn't easy. I mean, we [students from women's colleges] felt so powerful, and then we get out and we're in this world, just fighting those battles for employment. I mean, the idea that [Clinch Valley] wouldn't employ me—I had as good an education as anybody teaching there, and I had published a lot more than anybody else after a few years, *and* my resume was better than theirs. I still couldn't be hired. I ran across those barriers and that just infuriated me, because I had expected [to succeed].

TAKING APPALACHIAN STUDIES STUDENTS
ON A TRIP TO NEW YORK IN 1969

I had people like Harry Caudill [Appalachian historian and author of *Night Comes to the Cumberlands*] and all these people coming to speak and students doing all these things, and we ended up going to hear [Joseph Yablonski, labor activist and unsuccessful candidate for presidency of the United Mine Workers Association]. I taught an urban sociology course. We had to deal with urban problems, and so we go to New York and stay and study the Puerto Rican immigration to New York.

While we're up there, the Young Lords had taken over this church, and they were like the Black Panthers. So they let us into the church they were taking over before the police had busted them, and they said, "Well, you know we probably will be busted by the police pretty soon and probably killed. Anybody that tries to do any change gets killed." And of course there was Martin Luther King, the

Kennedys—all that had happened by then. We get up to Times Square and go into this record shop, and they're playing "Oh Death," which is a Dock Boggs piece, and Dock [an Appalachian songwriter and banjo player] is one of our neighbors. He had been in my classes some and been interviewed by the class about his coalmining and his coalmining songs. Then we walk out and [hear] the news that Yablonski and his wife and daughter had been killed.

It looked like the assassins probably had come from our district, because it was a big Boyle district. [W. A. "Tony" Boyle was the president of the UMWA, Yablonski's opponent in the presidential race, and later found to have hired the gunmen who killed Yablonski.] Because I had taken students up to hear Yablonski speak—I mean, the students and I sat up all night long in the Y where we were staying, talking about it. If you had planned any educational experience to shock your students you couldn't have done better. It was just incredible that all those things happened right there. It affected all the students—every one of them.

THE HIGHLANDER FOLK SCHOOL, THE CIVIL RIGHTS MOVEMENT, AND ECONOMIC EDUCATION

I had heard about Highlander even when I was in college but had never been part of it, and, being in Appalachia during the really hot times of the Civil Rights Movement, we were too busy fighting the coal companies.[6] I wasn't at Selma, I didn't walk across that bridge, I didn't go for the Mississippi Summer, I was not involved. My Civil Rights stuff was early. It was in the '40s, when people don't know that there was anything going on. So I was [at Highlander] for the Appalachian period and on into the times when we were trying to pull together the Civil Rights South people and the Appalachian people—and that was the last phase—and then integrating in the new immigrants and the Spanish[-language] immigrants.

[Longtime southern activist Sue Thrasher] and I went up to [the University of Massachusetts at Amherst] and took that radical economics course that they have there in the summer. We checked out every program in the country, got all the syllabi together, and all of them didn't really fit us. The Amherst thing was great for people who already had an economics major or were college educated, but it was not for ordinary country people with a seventh-grade education, even high school education. So we decided to go back to our form of education and see what we could do in terms of economic education based on [the] Highlander style of people learning from each other.

People are storytellers. People like to tell stories, so we developed a curriculum which could be used in some of these outreach programs. One of the things that I and other people were doing was develop little education programs, like in Dungannon, Virginia. We developed a GED program, and then we talked Mountain Empire Community College into offering some college courses there. They

"There are certain things you have to do. You're going to get in trouble, but that's all right. [Highlander's co-founder] Myles Horton always said, 'You're better known by the enemies you make.'" Photograph courtesy of Helen Matthews Lewis (center).

agreed to try out our little program, a class that we would have on learning your economic history. So we taught a class there, and [labor activist and historian] John Gaventa and I taught one at [the community center at Jellico, Tennessee] later.

It all grew out of our developing this thing where we start with oral histories, and what we start with is *what did your grandparents do to make a living?* And *what did your parents do to make a living?* And *what do you do to make a living, and what does your generation make a living doing?* And then we analyzed the history of the economy of this community and how it has changed, and you come up with actually a history of the economic changes in the United States, even with a small group of people. Even in these isolated places people have migrated out to get jobs, migrated in to get jobs, been involved in all the various changes that have occurred in the economy. Then we get to the point of *What is our economy today? Where does the money come from? Who has the money?*

I think it had to do with principles of equality and fairness and justice, and where I got all of that. Part of it was through religion. Part of it was through my father, who was a very just, caring person, and my mother, who was a really hard-working, loving person. And things I read. I read about powerful women, strong women. I was a great admirer of Eleanor Roosevelt.

I felt I had to do it. There are certain things you have to do. You're going to get in trouble, but that's all right. [Highlander's co-founder] Myles Horton always said, "You're better known by the enemies you make."

NOTES

1. The photograph was taken in 1966 while Lewis was doing research on coal mining safety for the Bureau of Mines. The smears of coal dust on her cheeks were applied after her first trip below ground as part of an initiation by local miners, mimicking the initiation male miners endured of being rolled in coal dust. Lewis was one of very few women allowed in a mine during this period. Prior to the lawsuits of the 1970s that opened up the industry, women were banned from entering mines because this was considered to bring bad luck. The custom was so rigidly enforced that during her work for the Bureau of Mines she was forced to employ male researchers to interview men in the mines, while she interviewed women and families above ground.

2. See Helen M. Lewis, Linda Johnson, and Don Askins, eds., *Colonialism in Modern America: The Appalachian Case* (Boone, NC: Appalachian Consortium Press, 1978).

3. Patricia Beaver, "An Interview with Helen Matthews Lewis," *Appalachian Journal* 15 (Spring 1988): 238–65.

4. "Appalachian Studies Programs: The General Philosophy Syllabus and Reading Lists," Research and Activism Series, Curriculum Subseries, Folder 2, Academic Papers, 1972–1986, Box 1, Helen Lewis Matthews Papers, Collection 103A, W. L. Eury Appalachian Collection, Appalachian State University.

5. Helen M. Lewis, Linda Selfridge, Juliet Merrifield, Sue Thrasher, Lillie Perry, and Carol Honeycutt, eds., "Picking Up the Pieces: Women In and Out of Work in the Rural South," (New Market, TN: Highlander Research and Education Center, 1986).

6. For more on the Highlander Center, see "I Train the People to Do Their Own Talking: Septima Clark and Women in the Civil Rights Movement," edited by Katherine Mellen Charron and David P. Cline, *Southern Cultures* 16, no. 2 (Summer 2010): 31–52.

Judge Thomas Ruffin and the Shadows of Southern History

by Sally Greene

Thomas Ruffin's statue, of heroic scale on a pedestal of polished white marble, makes a commanding presence, even from the alcove of the court building. Dressed in swallow-tail coat and cravat, Ruffin stands with an "air of power and of elevation." His squarely frontal yet unguarded position invokes a classical style of "ideal masculinity" that was refined in the eighteenth century. Photograph courtesy of the North Carolina Office of Archives and History, Raleigh, North Carolina.

visitor to the North Carolina Court of Appeals could be forgiven for failing to notice Judge Thomas Ruffin's statue in an alcove in the building's foyer. Obstructed by a latter-day handicap access ramp, the larger-than-life bronze figure nevertheless stolidly presides. From its opening in 1914 until 1940, this building was the home of the North Carolina Supreme Court, of which Ruffin was chief justice from 1833 to 1852. After 1940, when the Supreme Court moved next door to a building constructed by the Works Progress Administration, the building became known as the Library Building; in 1967, it became home to the newly established Court of Appeals.[1]

Ruffin's statue was created by Francis H. Packer, a New York artist of some renown who had studied with Saint-Gaudens. One of his statues already graced Union Square, as the lawn of the capitol is called. It depicts Worth Bagley, son of prominent North Carolinians and the first American officer killed in the Spanish-American War. As historian Gaines Foster has persuasively written, this war served as a powerful antidote to the Civil War, rallying the reunified nation to a common cause. Bagley's death, Catherine Bishir notes, "was hailed in the national press as sealing the 'covenant of brotherhood between north and south.'" The monument's inscription, FIRST FALLEN, 1898, echoed that of the nearby Confederate monument, FIRST AT BETHEL, LAST AT APPOMATTOX. The threads of American history thus came together in these monuments, as well as others near the capitol, to be joined, only a few years later, by the statue of Ruffin, the state's most distinguished jurist.[2]

The appearance of all of these monuments in Raleigh around the turn of the century reflected a local response to a sweeping national phenomenon. "[T]he decades between 1870 and 1910 comprised the most notable period in all of American history for erecting monuments in honor of mighty warriors, groups of unsung heroes, and great deeds," writes Michael Kammen in *The Mystic Chords of Memory*. "The movement carried with it a kind of 'contagion' that spilled from Civil War saints to battles and martyrs of other wars." Although the poverty of the South after the war meant that the monuments there were slow in coming, the political elite throughout the region poured substantial resources into the business of memorialization.[3]

In North Carolina, the creation of what Bishir aptly calls "landmarks of power" took place in two phases. From the 1880s into the 1890s, the focus of the memorial movement shifted from cemeteries, where statues of fallen soldiers spoke a language of grief that transcended sectional loyalties, to public spaces, as dutiful citizens heeded a more partisan call. This period culminated in 1895, with the erection on Union Square of the 75-foot monument to the state's Confederate dead. The second phase came in reaction to an unexpected political development: in 1894 and 1896, the Democrats lost control of the legislature and the governorship to a

"Fusion" ticket backed by Populists and Republicans. The response to this embarrassment was swift and sharp. In 1898, the Democrats rushed back into power on a platform of white supremacy, leaving a trail of violence, most notably the deadly coup d'état in Wilmington. In 1900 the party reclaimed the governorship and enlisted Jim Crow to seal the victory.[4]

Against this backdrop, the second phase of monument building reflected a "remarkable sense of shared purpose," Bishir observes. "With competing visions of the state's past, present, and future all but silenced in official discourse, leaders shared a powerful sense that both in politics and in the culture at large, matters had been returned to their correct alignment." In ways that resonated with the broader narrative of the Lost Cause, the state's history was reinterpreted as a tapestry of "old family heritage, Anglo-Saxon supremacy, and military and political heroism"; these were the fundamentals that would inspire "a rebirth of southern progress and leadership in the nation." Civil War governor Zebulon B. Vance was honored in 1900 with a statue placed high on a pedestal at the east entrance of the capitol (a project delayed by recent political upheavals in the state). Worth Bagley's widely celebrated memorial took its place on the square in 1907. Five years later, on a nearby spot, the United Daughters of the Confederacy placed a statue of Henry Lawson Wyatt, the "First Confederate Soldier to Fall in the Battle of the War Between the States," created by Gutzon Borglum, the famed artist of Mount Rushmore. Confederate veteran Ashley Horne's memorial to the North Carolina Women of the Confederacy, which faced outward from the square toward the Supreme Court building, was unveiled in June 1914.[5]

The idea of a statue honoring Thomas Ruffin (1787–1870) came out of this context of renewed pride and reflection. Ruffin was revered for his significant contributions to the state's legal doctrines, notably his use of the law to hasten economic progress. His precedent-setting opinion in *Raleigh and Gaston Railroad Company v. Davis* (1837) permitted railroads and other private corporations that served the public interest to benefit from eminent domain, thus ensuring that private interests did not oppose the expansion of the railroads or other infrastructure improvements. For this extension of the law to promote economic development, Ruffin is still praised. Moreover, as historians continue to acknowledge, the legal talent and personal integrity of Judge Ruffin, combined with the efforts of his similarly honorable colleague William Gaston, were key to the very survival of the court in the 1830s in the face of a populist legislature that threatened to dissolve it.[6]

Although he did not serve the Confederacy as a soldier like Henry Lawson Wyatt, Ruffin was ideologically sympathetic to the Confederate cause and remained so to his death. In one of his earliest opinions for the Supreme Court, he bolstered the authority of slaveowners by granting them practically limitless powers of discipline over their slaves: "The power of the master must be absolute," Ruffin wrote in *State v. Mann* (1829), "to render the submission of the slave perfect."

From the 1880s into the 1890s, the focus of the memorial movement in North Carolina shifted from cemeteries, where statues of fallen soldiers spoke a language of grief that transcended sectional loyalties, to public spaces, as dutiful citizens heeded a more partisan call. This period culminated in 1895, with this 75-foot monument to the state's Confederate dead on Union Square. Photograph courtesy of the North Carolina Office of Archives and History, Raleigh, North Carolina.

State v. Mann became the most notorious opinion in the entire body of slavery law—as well known to northern abolitionists, who considered the opinion emblematic of everything wrong with the slaveholding South, as it was to slave owners, who found its rhetoric emboldening. Ruffin's role in strengthening the institution of slavery by immunizing slave masters from criminal charges of cruelty received no mention at the statue's dedication, although the speakers, and most likely their audience, would surely have borne it in mind.[7]

A consideration of the history of his statue should suggest not so much an attempt to upset its foundation as an interest in enlarging our understanding of what it represents. It marks one brief chapter in the history of the reassertion of white dominance in the South after the Civil War—a story of national reunification that, through the very strength of its imagery, rendered the call for racial justice almost incomprehensible. Even so, within the contours of this narrative of Anglo-Saxon triumph can be found another one of resistance and refusal. The emancipationist counter-narrative, which never conceded its own irrelevance, survives as a reminder of the strength and resilience of generations of Americans committed to equal justice under the Constitution. A recognition of this counter-narrative has the potential to change the way we view Ruffin's statue: the statement of the fixed and irrefutable power of law that it was no doubt intended to make unfolds into a conversation about the uses of law by the powerful. Such a shift of perspective, in turn, invites us into a broader reconsideration of our ways of navigating the contested terrain of public commemorative art.

THE MONUMENT AND THE MAN

Monuments in public spaces, especially those placed at the seat of government, ask to be interpreted as tangible evidence of a people's values, with the expectation that they have been created through public processes, with public funding. But such is not always the case. The reigning fiction, according to Kirk Savage, is that these "volunteer enterprises sponsored by associations of 'public-spirited' citizens" reflected the genuine voice of "the people"—that those who brought such projects forward "were merely agents of a more universal collective whose shared memory the project embodied." The reality was that the process of commemoration was guided by the self-interest of the dominant class. Judge Ruffin's statue was no different, and as with virtually all memorials of the period, the honoree's family and members of the political elite—in this instance the North Carolina Bar Association—promoted and funded the statue.[8]

Correspondence between Packer and members of the committee in charge of the statue's placement and presentation reveals no competition or controversy over its design, a common conflict between artists and their patrons. Rather, the most contentious point turned out to be its location. Originally intended to join the statues of Vance, Wyatt, and Bagley on Union Square, its siting became an issue after Colonel Horne managed to "preempt" what was thought the best choice by securing the site facing the court building for his memorial to the Confederate women. If the monument to North Carolina's preeminent judge could not face the court building, its backers finally concluded after considering other locations on the square, then the court building itself—just opened for business in 1914—would make a fine showcase. Meanwhile, Packer continued to fashion the work in bronze, following the original plan for an outdoor location.[9]

At the dedication ceremony on February 1, 1915, Henry G. Connor, federal judge for the eastern district of North Carolina and chair of the placement and presentation committee, stressed the importance of keeping memory alive through physical likenesses: "Inspiration to higher and nobler lives, we are taught, is imparted not alone by the story of the life and work of the great and good, but in the preservation of their form and feature by the art of the painter and the sculptor."[10]

J. Crawfurd Biggs, president of the bar association, similarly emphasized the importance of placing the likenesses of the state's great historical figures on public display:

We have not exerted ourselves to stimulate a healthy State pride, by preserving in marble and bronze the records of the past, by erecting statues and suitable memorials to commemorate the name and fame of the great men whose services have enriched and glorified the traditions of our Commonwealth. It is from the experience of the past that we draw inspiration for the future, and any act which emblazons in imperishable form the great deeds of our ancestors should be regarded with favor.[11]

Accepting the statue for the state, Governor Locke Craig mixed colonialist and Enlightenment rhetoric to underscore the broad reach of Ruffin's reputation:

He is recognized everywhere as one of the greatest judges that our race has produced. In the uttermost parts of the earth, where the English jurisprudence exercises its beneficent rule, he speaks and will speak to legislatures, to courts, and to executives, directing and enlightening them in the way of truth and in the conception and the administration of justice.[12]

The statue, of heroic scale on a pedestal of polished white marble, makes a commanding presence, even from the alcove of the court building. Working from photographs provided by the Ruffin family, Packer rendered the judge's "form and feature" in an iconography well suited to a man born, as Ruffin himself had once famously noted, "before the Constitution was adopted." Dressed in swallow-tail coat and cravat, just as Episcopal bishop Joseph Cheshire remembered him as an old man at St. Matthew's Church in nearby Hillsborough, he stands erect, with an "air of power and of elevation." His squarely frontal yet unguarded position

The second phase of monument building resonated with the broader narrative of the Lost Cause. During this era, in 1912, the United Daughters of the Confederacy placed this statue of Henry Lawson Wyatt (the "First Confederate Soldier to Fall in the Battle of the War Between the States"), which was created by Gutzon Borglum, the famed artist of Mount Rushmore. Photograph courtesy of the North Carolina Office of Archives and History, Raleigh, North Carolina.

invokes a classical style of "ideal masculinity" that was refined in the eighteenth century. Discussing this iconic tradition as it evolved through the period of J. A. Houdon's statue of George Washington (a copy of which was the first statue to be erected on Union Square, in 1857), artist and critic Anthea Callen writes that the pose "communicates an expansive openness; but it is not open in the sense of receptive, rather of complacent self-assurance." Consistent with this tradition, Ruffin's eyes are cast downward in such a way as to suggest introspection, knowledge, and authority—intimations of "man's enlightened state."[13]

In his left hand is a symbol of his office, sealed legal papers secured with a clasp imprinted with the scales of justice. His right hand is tucked inside his waistcoat, a gesture common among men of high social status in eighteenth-century English portraiture. The "hand-in-waistcoat" pose invokes a long tradition of which Jacques-Louis David's portrait of Napoleon offers perhaps the most famous example. Over the course of the century, this pose, which ultimately derived from within the tradition of classical sculpture, came to be "considered eminently suited to the taste of 'persons of quality and worth,'" according to art historian Arline Meyer. Its use became widespread "at the critical juncture when England was emerging as a national power" through a series of wars with France; in fact, the gesture contributed to what evolved as the English national style: "'manly boldness tempered with modesty.'"[14]

In a post–Civil War context, the iconography of classical sculpture itself was freighted with racial implications. In support of an argument for the hierarchy of the races, a popular "scientific" treatise of the day by Josiah Nott and George R. Gliddon, *Types of Mankind* (1854), included an illustration with a bust of Apollo on top, an exaggerated "Negro" head in the middle, and that of a chimpanzee on the bottom. The Apollo was taken from the Apollo Belvedere, a celebrated marble sculpture of Classic Antiquity, long considered the model of aesthetic perfection. That the epitome of aesthetic perfection was white in this era goes without saying, and the statues fashioned on this aesthetic became part of a language of whiteness and, thus, racial superiority. "More than any of the other arts," writes Savage, "sculpture was embedded in the theoretical foundation of racism that supported American slavery and survived long after its demise." In conforming to the conventions of classical sculpture, the statue of Judge Ruffin implicitly reinforced the assumption of the day that culture and education were associated with whiteness alone.[15]

"THE ABLEST JUDGE WHO HAS EVER PRESIDED IN THIS STATE"

In his keynote address at the statue's dedication—with rhetoric as lofty as the occasion demanded—Chief Justice Walter Clark sang the manifold accomplishments of one whose "fame as a Judge is established wherever the English law is known." Winding to his conclusion, Clark invited the audience to "[l]ook at his tall, sinewy figure as you shall soon see it, in monumental bronze; his firm mouth; his nose like an eagle's beak, his flashing eyes. He was a man of iron will, a man of determination, a man who would not be denied. He was every inch a man among men." Francis Packer had translated Ruffin the man into the classical language of patriarchal authority, skillfully communicating a lasting image of "elevated power and civic *gravitas*" that well suited the temper of the time.[16]

Ruffin's reputation as "the ablest Judge who has ever presided in this State," in Clark's words, survived well into the first half of the twentieth century. Writing in 1919 on the one-hundredth anniversary of the North Carolina Supreme Court, prominent attorney Robert W. Winston called him "the stern and clear-minded prophet." Ruffin's decisions on economic development issues earned lasting praise for helping North Carolina shed its reputation as "the Rip Van Winkle of the States." In an important history of antebellum North Carolina published in 1937, Guion Johnson confirmed that Ruffin's strong presence as chief justice was instrumental to the survival of the independent judiciary against pressures of democratic reform. He garnered widespread praise for his contributions to the law of equity, which is fairness itself. Nationally, Ruffin joined the ranks of John Marshall, Joseph Story, James Kent, and other distinguished jurists as authors of the American constitutional tradition.[17]

Perhaps most significantly, in 1938 the eminent legal scholar Roscoe Pound elevated Ruffin to the pantheon of judges whose faithful adherence to the common-law tradition instituted the "formative era" of American law. Although a fuller discussion of Pound's praise within the context of his own career would suggest that he was motivated by his own conservative self-interest, his claim unquestionably played a key role in protecting Ruffin's reputation from the ideological challenges of the mid-twentieth century.[18] By the end of the 1960s, however, as the Civil Rights Movement and the war in Vietnam confronted legal scholars with perplexing questions about the intersection of law and morality, "the tragic depth of the history of the law of slavery" began to reveal itself, recalls Stanley Katz. At the University of Chicago in 1974, Katz had played host to the first academic conference on the law of slavery. At the center of it all, he remembered some twenty years later, lay an opinion written by Thomas Ruffin:

> It was as though a group of people who had never seen one another before discovered that they had all been raised in the same little village. This village was intensely remembered although differently understood. It was named *State v. Mann*, which nearly all of us identified as the central text in the field, for the incredible manner in which Judge Thomas Ruffin, one of the great (and otherwise admirable) state judges of the nineteenth century, laid out the logic of slave law as coolly as a surgeon slicing open the belly of a patient on the operating table.

Confederate veteran Ashley Horne's memorial to the North Carolina Women of the Confederacy, unveiled in June 1914, faced outward from the square toward the Supreme Court building, "preempting" what was thought the best choice of site for the Ruffin statue. Photograph courtesy of the North Carolina Office of Archives and History, Raleigh, North Carolina.

Sanford Levinson, also in attendance, wondered whether Ruffin's "egregious" opinion should deprive him of such a reverential honor as, for example, having his portrait displayed in an American law school "as a presumed inspiration." Although more recent scholarship has broadened the discussion of the jurisprudence of slavery to show that what transpired in the highest courts was only part of the picture—that the law itself was shaped from the bottom up by distinctly local concerns—*State v. Mann* continues to hold a singular pride of place.[19]

STATE V. MANN

In this appeal from a trial in Edenton in 1829, the North Carolina Supreme Court reversed a jury's conviction of a slave's hirer for shooting the slave as she fled to avoid his whipping. Writing for the court, Ruffin declared that John Mann, the hirer, commanded mastery over Lydia, the slave, with "absolute" powers of discipline. Short of acting with intent to kill, this case appeared to say, the master would not incur criminal liability for any degree of correction. What gives pause is the stark reasoning that Ruffin employs to describe the workings of slavery. In the lower court, the jury's finding of guilt had not been altogether surprising: an assault upon a slave owned by someone else was a serious criminal offense. Ruffin, however, applied a rigorously structural understanding of the power relations involved. Mann may not have owned Lydia, but he owned the right to use her for the term of his contract. During that time, Ruffin reasoned, Mann had acquired all of the rights and privileges (such as they were) of the owner. Even as he professed anguish that this case had come to court, Ruffin presented the law as if it were unyielding. The master's power must be "absolute." Neither duty nor pleasure compels a slave to remain a slave, he observed: the slave's loyalty "is the consequence only of uncontrolled authority over the body." Unfettered power in the hands of the master—even a temporary "master"—was in Ruffin's view a necessary rule of law.[20]

In its own time, *State v. Mann* gained wide circulation. Slave hirers as well as owners throughout the state interpreted the opinion as giving them a wide berth. The brother of Harriet Jacobs, author of *Incidents in the Life of a Slave Girl* (1861), recalled an incident in which a Chowan County hirer cruelly punished a slave with impunity, attributing his behavior to the rule laid down in Ruffin's opinion. The civil rights activist Pauli Murray learned from her grandmother Cornelia, who was both the slave and the niece of Mary Ruffin Smith of Orange County, that Ruffin's insistence on "a master's absolute right over his slave's person" worked to sanction the sexual violence that Cornelia's mother suffered at the hands of Mary's brothers. Citing a particularly brutal incident from Raleigh in which an enslaved woman's master had caused her to be tied up with rope and dragged through the

"The power of the master must be absolute," Ruffin wrote in State v. Mann *(1829), "to render the submission of the slave perfect."* State v. Mann *became the most notorious opinion in the entire body of slavery law — as well known to northern abolitionists, who considered the opinion emblematic of everything wrong with the slaveholding South, as it was to slave owners, who found its rhetoric emboldening. Portrait of Thomas Ruffin, courtesy of the North Carolina Collection Photographic Archives, Wilson Library, UNC-Chapel Hill.*

streets by a horse, Harriet Beecher Stowe maintained that *State v. Mann* licensed unspeakable abuse.[21]

Stowe was the most prominent of the abolitionists who took Ruffin's unflinching description of the power dynamics of slavery as certain proof of its immorality. She was so bewildered by the opinion that she incorporated it into a novel, *Dred: A Tale of the Great Dismal Swamp*. Published in 1856, four years after *Uncle Tom's Cabin*, it is a much more searing critique of the chattel slave system. If, in the earlier novel, Stowe is content to imply that getting past slavery is just a matter of getting one's heart in the right place, this time she squarely confronts the social structure. She blames judges, lawyers, politicians, and ministers for standing in the way of reform. In her rewriting of *State v. Mann*, the prosecutor whose trial-court victory is overturned is the judge's own son, who responds to the decision by renouncing the bar and taking his slaves to Canada. Consistent with her ideological project of advocating a "higher law" theory of racial justice, Stowe's thinly fictionalized Judge Ruffin is an essentially just man compelled by the immutable logic of an imperfect legal system to reach a heinous conclusion. Reinterpreted thus by the most popular American writer of the time, *State v. Mann* found an expanded and highly critical audience.[22]

Into the early twentieth century, when North Carolina's elite was doing its best to recast its legal history in an unbroken celebration of political freedom from the Colonial period forward, *State v. Mann* figured usefully in the alternative histories of black Americans. Speaking on the topic of "Reconstruction and Its Benefits," W. E. B. Du Bois began a speech to the American Historical Association in 1909 with an ironic reference to Ruffin's opinion (and perhaps Stowe's novel as well). Life in the South after the devastation of the war would have been hard enough even "if there had not been a single freedman left," he said; but given the reality of four million freedmen, each of them—here he quoted from *State v. Mann*— "'doomed in his own person, and his posterity, to live without knowledge, and without the capacity to make anything his own, and to toil that another may reap the fruits,'" each one "is bound, on sudden emancipation, to loom like a great dread on the horizon." In an essay published the same year, Booker T. Washington criticizes the emphasis that Ruffin places on "the profit of the master, his security, and the public safety" as the proper end of the master-slave relationship. With such reasoning, writes Washington, "This opinion brings out into plain view an idea that was always somewhere at the bottom of slavery—the idea, namely, that one man's evil is another man's good." But the truth about slavery, he counters, is "just the opposite . . . namely, that evil breeds evil, just as disease breeds disease, and that a wrong committed upon one portion of a community will, in the long run, surely react upon the other portion of that community."[23]

And yet, despite the persistent criticism that ran from the literature of the abolitionists through the later discourse of African American letters, Judge Ruffin continued to stand tall in official Raleigh well into the 1960s—even against the backdrop of the Greensboro sit-ins and the tumultuous struggle for civil rights that followed. In fact, the court building where the statue is housed was formally named the "Ruffin Building" in 1969. Within months after the new name went up on the building, a class of Raleigh junior high students noticed the statue of this great man with the very scales of justice weighing in his hands. They wanted it taken out of the shadows and moved across the street to Union Square, and they managed to persuade the state legislature to pass a resolution asking that it be done. This they took to the Capital Planning Commission, which appeared sympathetic until learning of the $15,000 cost, which prompted it to seek a higher authority. In February 1970, the state Supreme Court rendered its decision: it preferred not to.[24]

Although the court's reasoning was opaque, an editorial in the Raleigh *News and Observer* of the time suggests that some public debate did take place. Titled "Pandora's Buildings," it notes certain "real questions as to where the statue of the great Thomas Ruffin should stand or whether the building in which it stands is properly and legally to be called the Ruffin Building." Though it might be an acceptable practice to "purchase a sort of immortality by philanthropy as is the case with the Reynolds Coliseum and the Carter Stadium"—or all of Duke University—the editorialist worried that among public buildings "the competition for structural immortality might get out of bounds." Some time later, the name "Ruffin" disappeared. The brass plaque bearing the name was long ago replaced by another marking simply the Court of Appeals Building (though lawyers of a certain age still call it the Ruffin Building). Reading between the lines of the story as reported might suggest that, given the politics of the civil rights movement, the Supreme Court wished to save itself and the state the embarrassment of calling attention to the author of the most strident, most telling justification of slavery in the entire body of antebellum American law. But it was not that way at all.[25]

Raymond Taylor, Supreme Court marshal and librarian from 1964 to 1977, recalls that the idea of moving Ruffin out of the Court of Appeals building emerged from the internal politics of the Supreme Court, which had called the "Ruffin Building" home until 1940, and the fledgling Court of Appeals, only two years old in 1969. Former Chief Justice Emery B. Denny, retired by that time "but still very much on the scene," according to Taylor, was troubled by some unfinished business. Upon his appointment to that court in the early 1940s, one of Denny's assignments had been to ensure that the court's artwork—portraits and sculpture memorializing former judges—was relocated to the new building. He succeeded with the portraits and busts, but more than twenty years later he was disappointed that the statue of Ruffin remained in the old court building. He wanted the statue relocated to a site on Union Square, directly facing the modern Supreme Court building. "There was not—and still is not—a jurist, a representative of the judicial branch, on the square," Taylor said. "Judge Denny wanted that done."[26]

A local architect confirmed that the statue could withstand the elements. The setting he designed for the proposed location positioned the judge's statue within a low circular wall, perhaps with a sitting space, with room for the names of all of the chief justices. "But a strange thing happened," Taylor said. "Mysteriously, almost under cover of darkness," in February 1969 "a sign appeared on the Court of Appeals [building], and it said the Ruffin Building."[27] A state official called the new name part of a "program of building identification" initiated by the governor. But only one building was identified by the name of a person. Taylor was unable to find any documentation regarding the decision, leading him eventually to believe that the Court of Appeals wanted to keep the statue and its members felt the chances were improved if the building bore Ruffin's name. "It was a matter of sheer political power that got that done," he concluded.[28]

Ann Kennedy's seventh-grade history students from LeRoy Martin Junior High were studying Thomas Ruffin when they began to read about Justice Denny's proposal to move the statue outside, Taylor recalled. After their enthusiastic support translated to success with the legislature, they made a field trip to the Supreme Court, where they presented Chief Justice R. Hunt Parker with a jar of money for the relocation fund. Caught off guard, he accepted the money but later asked Taylor to return it, which was a great disappointment to the children. Parker offered no explanation, but whatever his reasoning, it surely did not involve anxiety about Ruffin's emerging academic reputation as the father of the law of slavery. The following excerpt from his 1968 annual report to the state bar demonstrates little concern that calling attention to Judge Ruffin might have been politically unwise at that moment:

> The world is traveling under formidable omens into a new era, an era no man can foresee, no man foretell. The country is undergoing more crime and violence than ever before in our history. The worst of our youngsters are growing up to become booted, sideburned, duck-tailed, unwashed, leather-jacketed beatniks and hippies; a large number of the best of our youth are coming into maturity for all the world like young people fresh from a dizzying roller-coaster ride with everything blurred, nothing clear, with no positive standards, with everything in doubt. An example of that is the turmoil and unrest in our colleges and universities wherein men with long hair and looking like women, and women with short hair dressed in pants looking like men are in the forefront of this unrest . . . Frequently, the news media and college professors and other adults with no practical experience in the hard, concrete facts of life are encour-

In a post–Civil War context, classical sculpture itself was freighted with racial implications. In support of a hierarchy of races, Josiah Nott and George R. Gliddon's "scientific" treatise, Types of Mankind *(1854), included an illustration that made preeminent a bust of the Apollo Belvedere, the celebrated marble sculpture of Classic Antiquity long considered the model of aesthetic perfection. That the epitome of aesthetic perfection was white during this era was no surprise, and statues fashioned on this aesthetic in turn became part of a language of whiteness and racial superiority.* Apollo Belvedere, Roman copy, 120–140 CE, after a Greek bronze original, 330–320 BCE, Museo Pio-Clementino, Rome, Italy, photographed by Marie-Lan Nguyen.

aging this disorder. In my opinion, and in the opinion of many others, all of this disorder is created and inspired by hard core Communists.

As Taylor observed in reflecting on this remarkable passage, the Chief Justice Parker was clearly "not in sympathy with anybody who would have objected to Thomas Ruffin."[29]

Fifteen years later, in 1984, another campaign sought to bring the statue outdoors, this time to the nearby Fayetteville Street Mall (then a pedestrian mall, now a traffic corridor). Even then, no discussion appears to have taken place about Ruffin's role in the history of slavery. Rather, this second effort, led by Labor Commissioner John C. Brooks, quickly devolved into another turf war, this one with battle lines clearly visible. Brooks pressed the issue with the city's Downtown Advisory Committee, but he overplayed his hand. The committee denied the request, taking the curious position that the mall, "with its flowers, trees and grass," was "inappropriate for a statue."[30]

So there he stands, the man who would not be moved, in the building that is, and is not, the Ruffin Building. Hurried lawyers scarcely notice Judge Ruffin as they file in and out of the Court of Appeals Building—so indelibly and for so long a fixture, he is simply ignored. In an Episcopal churchyard in Hillsborough, Judge Ruffin's gravestone makes its own contribution to the cause of national re-unification that the statue, taking its place near the others on Union Square, was designed to promote. Inscribed on his classical obelisk is this couplet: "A man resolved, and steady to his trust, / Inflexible to ill, and obstinately just." Ruffin's early twentieth-century memorializers recognized how perfectly this verse, from Addison's translation of a Horatian ode, suited the man (there was talk of repeating it on the statue). It happens that the same words once described George Washington.[31]

"THE PRESENT IS BURDENED TOO MUCH WITH THE PAST"

For all his ideological investment in the slaveholding world of the nineteenth century, Thomas Ruffin is fundamentally a child of Washington's time. Born in the eighteenth century, he gave his life to the law, to a particular kind of law in which rigorous discipline was bound up with equally uncompromising notions of habit and duty, honor and piety. For the cultivation of those classical virtues, the reliable exercise of memory proved essential. Gentlemen trained in the traditions inherited from eighteenth-century England used the tools of memory to classify and "methodize" their thoughts as they conformed their behavior to society's norms. But somewhere between Ruffin's well-ordered world and ours, the ground shifted. With the rise of Romanticism and modernism, the function of memory itself became problematic, opening the way to new understandings of its relationship to order, and thus to history. Questions we have learned to ask about the role of historical memory—about the shape-shifting ways in which memory travels through various sources of cultural authority—are essentially modern questions. Inquiries posed by William Wordsworth and Samuel Taylor Coleridge into the nature of memory found more urgent expression in the works of Henri Bergson and Marcel Proust, who spurned the kind of memory that was synonymous with habitual behavior—what Bergson called a "closed system of automatic movements"—and sought, rather, to encourage a subjective engagement with memory, even to the extent of rejecting memory as an impediment to creativity.[32]

From this perspective, Freud, speaking before an American audience, contended that forgetting the past was sometimes advisable:

> [W]hat should we think of a Londoner who paused today in deep melancholy before the memorial of Queen Eleanor's funeral instead of going about his business? . . . Or again, what should we think of a Londoner who shed tears be-

Ruffin's State v. Mann *decision and its emphasis on "the profit of the master, his security, and the public safety" figured in a 1909 Booker T. Washington essay: "This opinion brings out into plain view an idea that was always somewhere at the bottom of slavery—the idea, namely, that one man's evil is another man's good." But the truth about slavery, wrote Washington, is "just the opposite . . . namely, that evil breeds evil, just as disease breeds disease, and that a wrong committed upon one portion of a community will, in the long run, surely react upon the other portion of that community." Booker T. Washington, ca. 1900, courtesy of the Collections of the Library of Congress.*

fore the Monument that commemorates the reduction of his beloved metropolis to ashes, although it has long since risen again in far greater brilliance? . . . Not only do they remember painful experiences of the remote past, but they still cling to them emotionally; they cannot get free of the past and for its sake they neglect what is real and immediate.

Here, Freud echoes Hawthorne, who, on seeing the Elgin Marbles, concluded that "[t]he present is burdened too much with the past. We have not time . . . to appreciate what is warm with life, and immediately around us."[33]

From the beginnings of the American experiment in democracy, as Michael

Kammen has amply demonstrated, the question of how to commemorate the new nation's past posed something of a paradox. "Democracy has no monuments," wrote John Quincy Adams. "It strikes no medals. It bears the head of no man on a coin." Although such radical idealism was never strictly put into practice in a country whose pioneers, after all, came from lands steeped in history and remembrance, it took the ordeal of the Civil War, as Kammen observes, "to minimize genuinely revolutionary aspects of the American Revolution" and to usher in "a conservative, organic view of society." In the North and throughout the vanquished South, the ravages of war provoked a longing for the stability offered by a sense of shared tradition.[34]

Out of the postwar impulse for a healing, anchoring narrative came the rhetoric of the Lost Cause. Faced with military defeat and the specter of four million former slaves, leaders and foot soldiers of the old Confederacy put their energies toward nothing less than writing the history of the war on their own terms—terms that embraced reconciliation and reunion with their foes—rather than engaging in the project of doing justice for the newly free. As historian David Blight has written, "the forces of reconciliation overwhelmed the emancipationist vision in the national culture," with the result that "the inexorable drive for reunion both used and trumped race." Through the hard years of Reconstruction and into the twentieth century, Blight further observes, the Lost Cause "came to represent a mood, or an attitude toward the past," for white southerners "a natural extension of evangelical piety, a civil religion that helped them link their sense of loss to a Christian conception of history." Across the southern landscape, the Lost Cause gained tangible legitimation in the form of public monuments and memorials, all telling a lofty tale of pride and patriotism and loyalty to abiding principles. The statue of Thomas Ruffin, with the others of its era on the grounds of the capitol in Raleigh, remains as a testament to this historical narrative.[35]

Ultimately, the social cohesion that came out of these common tropes of memory could no longer hold—undone by the insistence of racial politics and the forces of modernity itself. In turn, a rhetorical practice grounded in longing was subjected to the peculiarly modern practice of historical criticism. Virginia Woolf, for example, teaches us how to cast a wary gaze. While "walking down Whitehall," she suggests, a woman might confront "a sudden splitting off of consciousness, . . . when from being the natural inheritor of that civilisation, she becomes, on the contrary, outside of it, alien and critical." With Bergson and Proust, she resists the automatic assent that a public monument is meant to compel. "Walk through the Admiralty Arch . . . or any other avenue given up to trophies and cannon," she advises, "and reflect upon the kind of glory celebrated there." Consider why the monuments were erected, she urges, and at what cost.[36]

If a campaign to bring Judge Ruffin out of the shadows and onto a more favorable site were to succeed today, the move would not pose a daunting logistical problem. The problem would be how to return his steady gaze. We might want to ask, as Harriet Beecher Stowe did, why he was content to be "merely an *expositor*, and not a *reformer* of law." Although he never sanctioned a violent response to the crisis of race—with relentless logic and fidelity to law he condemned the Ku Klux Klan for undertaking "an attempt to do good by wrong means"—we might be tempted to lay more than a century of bloodshed before him as a rational consequence of his work to strengthen a system of human bondage. We might ask him to consider the continuum of history that links his part in securing "the power of the master" to the powerful witness of artifacts from the lunch counter sit-ins of the 1960s that are found in the nearby North Carolina Museum of History.[37]

In fact, it would be a pleasure to help Judge Ruffin down from his pedestal and take him on a short walk past the museum, up Wilmington Street to the corner of East Lane Street. On that site, now a parking lot situated behind the state archives and across the street from the Legislative Building, a new historical monument is planned. Years in the making and still in the fundraising stage, the North Carolina Freedom Monument promises to be a space for reflection suited to our own time—responsive to the regrets and sorrows, the hopes and longings that filter our thoughts about the ways in which race continues to shape our history.

The word "monument" deceives. What is contemplated is not a single statue or form designed to convey a single message. The statues of Ruffin, Bagley, and others near the capitol are figures of outsize proportion that ask us to "accept the memory of [the state] as our own," as Howard Zinn put it, "conceal[ing] fierce conflicts of interest (sometimes exploding, most often repressed) between conquerors and conquered, masters and slaves, capitalists and workers, dominators and dominated in race and sex." The design of the Freedom Monument, in contrast, incorporates "a series of engaging sculptural experiences seamlessly integrated with the landscape." Multiple elements will represent broad themes of the African American freedom struggle: ingenuity and resilience, tension, and hope.[38]

Visitors will find their own paths through an intriguing landscape that features informal clusters of shade trees, evoking the "freedom groves" where slaves would gather to learn from each other. Comfortable reading benches will be situated under the trees, while in the open plaza jagged benches will suggest memories of turbulent times. Children will play hopscotch on pavers etched with the words "Not Every Step Is Sure." Vistas will be deliberately obscured by the Jim Crow Wall, which, like the system it represents, will require careful negotiation. Eastern North Carolina, where most of the state's slaves lived, will be remembered in the Serpentine Wall, its undulating lines evoking the ocean shores where their ances-

The word "monument" deceives. What is contemplated is not a single statue or form designed to convey a single message. The statues of Ruffin, Bagley, and others near the capitol are figures of outsize proportion that ask us to "accept the memory of [the state] as our own," as Howard Zinn put it, to "conceal fierce conflicts of interest (sometimes exploding, most often repressed) between conquerors and conquered, masters and slaves, capitalists and workers, dominators and dominated in race and sex." Four Pueblo men (left to right: Santiago Naranjo, Waihusing, James Miller, and Jesus Baca), each carrying a cane given them by Abraham Lincoln as a token of promise of permanent retention of their lands, 1923, courtesy of the Collections of the Library of Congress.

tors first arrived. Perhaps Judge Ruffin would join us on the Freedom Steps, the site's highest elevation, as we observe others making their way down the spiraling walkways, or reacting to the provocative setting, or paused in quiet contemplation. We will do our best to take it all in, knowing that though we can never rise above our history, some vantage points yield clearer views than others—knowing, too, that no matter how many views we can claim, no matter how expansive, another prospect always beckons.[39]

The author would like to thank John Sanders for research assistance on Packer and the story of the Ruffin statue's creation, Tom Davis of the North Carolina Supreme Court Library for further research assistance, and Catherine Bishir and Ayse Erginer for careful editorial advice. A version of this essay will appear in *Commemoration in America: Essays on Monuments, Memorialization, and Memory*, edited by E. G. Daves Rossell and David W. Gobel (forthcoming, University of Virginia Press, 2012).

1. *"Curia Passim": A Brief History of the Sites of the North Carolina Supreme Court*, brochure (Raleigh: State of North Carolina, 1993).

2. John Sanders, "Francis Herman Packer," *Dictionary of North Carolina Biography*, ed. William S. Powell (Chapel Hill: University of North Carolina Press, 1994), 5:1; Gaines M. Foster, *Ghosts of the Confederacy: Defeat, the Lost Cause, and the Emergence of the New South 1865 to 1913* (New York: Oxford University Press, 1987), 145; Catherine Bishir, "Landmarks of Power: Building a Southern Past in Raleigh and Wilmington, North Carolina, 1885-1915," in *Where These Memories Grow: History, Memory, and Southern Identity*, ed. W. Fitzhugh Brundage (Chapel Hill: University of North Carolina Press, 2000), 150-51.

3. Michael Kammen, *Mystic Chords of Memory: The Transformation of Tradition in American Culture* (New York: Knopf, 1991), 115.

4. Bishir, "Landmarks of Power," 143; on the shift from cemeteries to public spaces, see Dennis Montagna, "A Monument for a New Century," *Army* 53, no. 7 (2003): 42-47; Bishir, "Landmarks of Power," 147.

5. Bishir, "Landmarks of Power," 148-54.

6. Timothy S. Huebner, *The Southern Judicial Tradition: State Judges and Sectional Distinctiveness, 1790-1890* (Athens: University of Georgia Press, 1999), 138-41; Walter F. Pratt Jr., "The Struggle for Judicial Independence in Antebellum North Carolina: The Story of Two Judges," *Law and History Review* 4, no. 1 (1986): 129-59.

7. *State v. Mann*, 13 N.C. 263 (1829).

8. Contract for Ruffin Memorial, December 20, 1912, in Thomas Ruffin Papers, PC 896, North Carolina State Archives, Raleigh; Kirk Savage, *Standing Soldiers, Kneeling Slaves: Race, War, and Monument in Nineteenth-Century America* (Princeton, NJ: Princeton University Press, 1997), 6-7; Contract for Ruffin Memorial, December 20, 1912, in Thomas Ruffin Papers, PC 896, North Carolina State Archives, Raleigh.

9. Letter, Walter Clark to Bennehan Cameron, June 16, 1913, in Walter Clark Papers, PC 8.12, North Carolina State Archives, Raleigh. See also letter, Judge Henry G. Connor to Walter Clark, Oct. 18, 1913, in Henry G. Connor Papers, Box 14, folder 220, Southern Historical Collection, University of North Carolina at Chapel Hill.

10. H. G. Connor, "Opening Remarks," in *Addresses at the Unveiling and Presentation to the State of the Statue of Thomas Ruffin by the North Carolina Bar Association: Delivered in the Hall of the House of Representatives, 1 February, 1915* (Raleigh, NC: Edwards & Broughton Printing Co., 1915), 5.

11. J. Crawford Biggs, "Presentation," in *Addresses at the Unveiling*, 24.

12. Locke Craig, "Acceptance," in *Addresses at the Unveiling*, 26.

13. The statue is seven feet tall, on a plinth of four inches. Letter, F. H. Packer to Walter Clark, January 11, 1914, Walter Clark Papers, PC 8.12, North Carolina State Archives, Raleigh. On the Ruffin family's communication with Packer, see Frank Nash to H. G. Connor, June 28, 1915, in Henry G. Connor Papers, Box 16, folder 245, Southern Historical Collection, University of North Carolina at Chapel Hill; Joseph Blount Cheshire, *Nonnulla: Memories, Stories, Traditions, More or Less*

Authentic (Chapel Hill: University of North Carolina Press, 1930), 121; Anthea Callen, "Ideal Masculinities: An Anatomy of Power," in *The Visual Culture Reader*, ed. Nicholas Mirzoeff (New York: Routledge, 2002), 611–12.

14. Arline Meyer, "Re-dressing Classical Statuary: The Eighteenth-Century 'Hand-in-Waistcoat' Portrait," *Art Bulletin* 77, no. 1 (1995): 49, 53.

15. Savage, *Standing Soldiers, Kneeling Slaves*, 8–11.

16. Walter Clark, "Thomas Ruffin," in *Addresses at the Unveiling*, 17, 22; Callen, "Ideal Maculinities," 613.

17. Clark, "Thomas Ruffin," 15; Robert W. Winston, "A Century of Law in North Carolina," from the "Proceedings of the North Carolina Bar Association in the Supreme Court Room, Raleigh, 4 January 1919, on the Occasion of the Centennial Celebration of the One Hundredth Anniversary of the Establishment of the Supreme Court of North Carolina," 176 N.C. 789 (1919); J. G. de Roulhac Hamilton, *Party Politics in North Carolina, 1835–1860* (Durham, NC: Seeman Printery, 1916), 26; Guion Griffis Johnson, *Ante-Bellum North Carolina: A Social History* (Chapel Hill: University of North Carolina Press, 1937), 642–43. See also Samuel A. Ashe, "Thomas Ruffin," *Biographical History of North Carolina from Colonial Times to the Present*, ed. Samuel A. Ashe (Greensboro, NC: Charles L. Van Noppen, 1906), 352–53; Clark, "Thomas Ruffin," 15–17.

18. Pound's appreciation for common-law analysis in the 1930s was part of a surprising shift: with the ascendancy of the New Deal, which as an early Progressive he would logically have supported, he became one of its vocal critics. The Depression led him to identify with the business establishment, now chafing under the rules of the new regulatory state. He saw the move toward particularized, agency-specific administrative procedures for managing conflict—a development he had once championed—as a reflection of a dangerous slide toward totalitarianism. In *The Formative Era of American Law*, Pound puts Ruffin in the service of a reactionary argument that, in the end, resulted in a substantial victory. The passage of the Administrative Procedure Act of 1946, which imposed a layer of consistent judicial process on federal agency decision-making, marked "the triumph," according to Mortin Horwitz, of a "legalist mindset" that the New Dealers had strenuously opposed. Pound, *The Formative Era of American Law* (Boston: Little, Brown, 1938), 4, note 2, 84–86, 28–29; Horwitz, *The Transformation of American Law, 1870–1960: The Crisis of Legal Orthodoxy* (New York: Oxford University Press, 1992), 217–31.

19. Stanley N. Katz, "Bondage, Freedom, and the Constitution: New Slavery Scholarship and Its Impact on Law and Legal Historiography: Opening Address," *Cardozo Law Review* 17 (1996): 1690; Sanford Levinson, "Allocating Honor and Acting Honorably: Some Reflections Provoked by the Cardozo Conference on Slavery," *Cardozo Law Review* 17 (1996): 1969.

20. *State v. Mann*, 13 N.C. 263 (1829). For a full discussion of *State v. Mann*, arguing that Ruffin's reversal was compelled by neither law nor precedent, see Sally Greene, "*State v. Mann* Exhumed," *North Carolina Law Review* 87 (2009): 701–55.

21. John S. Jacobs, *A True Tale of Slavery*, in Harriet A. Jacobs, *Incidents in the Life of a Slave Girl, Written by Herself*, ed. Jean Fagan Yellin (New York: Harper's, 1987), 225–26, 226 note 50; Pauli Murray, *Proud Shoes: The Story of an American Family*, 2ⁿᵈ ed. (1978; repr., Boston, MA: Beacon Press, 1999), 45–46. Citations refer to the Beacon Press edition. Harriet Beecher Stowe, *A Key to Uncle Tom's Cabin* (1853; repr., Bedford, MA: Applewood Books, 1998), 104–06.

22. Stowe, *A Key to Uncle Tom's Cabin*, 77–79; *Dred: A Tale of the Great Dismal Swamp*, ed. Judie Newman (1856; repr., Edinburgh: Edinburgh University Press, 1999).

23. Reprinted in W. E. B. Du Bois, "Reconstruction and Its Benefits," *American Historical Review* 15 (1910): 781; Booker T. Washington, "The Negro's Life in Slavery," *Outlook*, September 11, 1909,

reprinted in the *Booker T. Washington Papers*, ed. Louis R. Harlan et al. (Urbana: University of Illinois Press, 1981), 163–64.

24. Jack Childs, "Will Thomas Ruffin Stay Inside?" [Raleigh] *News & Observer*, January 11, 1970, 15; Rod Cockshutt, "State Supreme Court Says Ruffin Should Stay in Place," [Raleigh] *News & Observer*, February 5, 1970, 44.

25. "Pandora's Buildings," editorial, [Raleigh] *News & Observer*, January 18, 1970, IV-4.

26. Raymond Taylor, interviewed by the author, April 7, 2003.

27. Taylor interview, April 2003.

28. Taylor interview, April 2003; "Building Gets a New Name," [Raleigh] *News & Observer*, February 21, 1969, 12; Taylor interview, April 2003.

29. Taylor interview, April 2003; "Remarks of Chief Justice R. Hunt Parker," *The North Carolina Bar* 15, no. 4 (1968): 27; Taylor interview, April 2003.

30. Kathy Tyndall, "Panel delays vote on moving ex-justice's statue," [Raleigh] *News & Observer*, February 2, 1984, C2; [Raleigh] *News & Observer*, "A turf war without a cause," February 7, 1984, A4; John Drescher Jr., "Statue called out of step for mall," [Raleigh] *News & Observer*, February 21, 1984, C1.

31. Joseph Addison's translation of Horace, Ode 3.3, is in *Miscellaneous Work in Verse and Prose of the Late Right Honourable Joseph Addison: With Some Account of the Life and Writings of the Author by Mr. Tickell* (London: Jacob Tonson, 1726), 142–47; for the debate about the wording to be on the statue, see letter from historian R. D. W. Connor to Frank Nash, July 8, 1914, and letter to Connor from his father, Henry G. Connor, July 17, 1914. R. D. W. Connor Papers, Box 2, folder 182, Southern Historical Collection, University of North Carolina at Chapel Hill; on Washington, see William Gaston, *Address Delivered before the Philanthropic and Dialectic Societies at Chapel Hill, June 20, 1832* (Raleigh, NC: Jos. Gales & Son, 1836), 7.

32. Lucia Dacome, "Noting the Mind: Commonplace Books and the Pursuit of the Self in Eighteenth-Century Britain," *Journal of the History of Ideas* 65, no. 4 (2004): 603–25; David Gross, *Lost Time: On Remembering and Forgetting in Late Modern Culture* (Amherst: University of Massachusetts Press, 2000), 30–31; Henri Bergson, *Matter and Memory* (1896), quoted in Gross, *Lost Time*, 42.

33. This passage from Freud's 1909 Clark University Lectures is quoted in Gross, *Lost Time*, 40–41; Hawthorne is quoted in Kammen, *Mystic Chords of Memory*, 40.

34. Adams is quoted in Kammen, *Mystic Chords of Memory*, 19; Kammen, *Mystic Chords of Memory*, 89.

35. David W. Blight, *Race and Reunion: The Civil War in American Memory* (Cambridge, MA: Harvard University Press, 2001), 2, 258.

36. Virginia Woolf, *A Room of One's Own* (1929; repr., New York: Harcourt Brace Jovanovich [Harvest], 1989), 97, 38.

37. Stowe, *A Key to Uncle Tom's Cabin*, 79; Ruffin, letter to son John K. Ruffin, July 8, 1869, *The Papers of Thomas Ruffin*, vol. 4, ed. J. G. de Roulhac Hamilton (Raleigh: North Carolina Historical Commission, 1920), 226.

38. Howard Zinn, *A People's History of the United States, 1492–Present* (1980; new ed., New York: Harper Perennial, 2005), 10.

39. Juan Logan, artist, with Lyneise Williams, art historian, and David Swanson, landscape architect, "North Carolina Freedom Monument Design Statement," 2009.

Hot Springs, Arkansas

by Keith Maillard

"Although the name of the town — Hot Springs, Arkansas — has been in my head for as long as words have been in there, it never occurred to me to think about the meaning of those words, to say to myself, 'Oh, there must be hot springs*' — as, indeed there are. The thermal waters flow from an ancient watershed at over 140 degrees Fahrenheit, but if my mother ever soaked herself in them, she never told me about it."* Men drinking mineral water at hot spring no. 29, ca. 1906, Hot Springs, Arkansas, courtesy of the Collections of the Library of Congress.

*A*lthough the name of the town—Hot Springs, Arkansas—has been in my head for as long as words have been in there, it never occurred to me to think about the meaning of those words, to say to myself, "Oh, there must be *hot springs*"—as, indeed there are. The thermal waters flow from an ancient watershed at over 140 degrees Fahrenheit, but if my mother ever soaked herself in them, she never told me about it. By the time that she and my father, Gene, were living there in 1942, the town had been transformed from a popular spa for folks with arthritis into a rehabilitation center for sick and wounded servicemen—but she never told me about that either. The Hot Springs I heard about is the town as she remembered it—a miserable rural dump in the middle of the ignorant, stinking hot, crapped-out, nowhere South. She agreed to go there with Gene, she told me, "to save the marriage."

There was no great love between us . . . either Gene for me or me for him. It was a matter of convenience at that point. I was pushing thirty and panicking. The fellas that I had run around with in Wheeling, I didn't want to marry. They were . . . stupid. I don't know. Gene had been around and in things. He was a different personality. We got along all right. But I couldn't live with his damned tight . . . His worshiping the dollar is what broke us up.

That is her summary, her official public statement delivered a lifetime later, but she also said, "Mother's the reason that your dad and I didn't get along," and even once, dropped as a sad aside while she was talking about something else, "I don't know what happened to us."

To say that they were trying "to save the marriage" implies that they'd talked about it, knew they were in trouble. I doubt that either she or Gene saw their marriage as "a matter of convenience"—at least not when they first went into it—but later, after it was over, she would hang that label on it to trivialize the experience, to push the pain away from her. The reason they split up is nothing that can be summarized in a few sentences. I grew up listening to her stories, and I don't believe that she ever really understood what happened in Hot Springs.

However much my father might have fancied himself an artist, a footloose entertainer, he liked his income to be reliable. Except for the last two years before the Crash—when he was playing comedic roles on the stage in Cleveland and then doing whatever he did in 1928—he always had a day gig. His first job of any consequence had been with the engineering firm of Sanderson & Porter in 1921. He worked elsewhere—most notably at Wheeling Steel—but Sanderson & Porter continued to employ him off and on for years. He must have proven himself as reliable to them as they had always been to him; wherever they needed him, he packed his suitcase and went—to half a dozen towns in Pennsylvania; to Lake Charles, Louisiana; to Biloxi, Mississippi; to Hot Springs, Arkansas.

I can find no record of Sanderson & Porter doing anything in Hot Springs, but as soon as the war started, they landed a fat government contract to build and operate the Pine Bluff facility sixty-three miles away. Magnesium and thermite incendiary bombs were manufactured, assembled, and stored at Pine Bluff. Just as the name implies, incendiary bombs are designed to set things on fire. Some of the bombs used to torch Dresden might well have been manufactured there.

Pine Bluff didn't have just a weapons plant; it had an arsenal and an airbase. The minute the word had gone out that the big bucks were coming to town, folks from all over Arkansas converged on Pine Bluff looking for work. They camped by the side of the road, crammed into boarding houses, as many as fourteen men to a room. When the plant was fully operational, over six thousand people were employed there, and there was no housing to be had. The situation got so bad that the Army Corps of Engineers towed quarter-boats up the Arkansas River from Memphis and stuffed a thousand workers into them. My parents didn't live in Pine Bluff, but that didn't necessarily mean that Gene wasn't working on the Pine Bluff project.

As a draftsman attached to the engineering department, Gene must have been one of the elite. The engineers might have set up offices in Hot Springs, close enough to Pine Bluff to send plans back and forth, or even commute when they had to, but well away from the overcrowded, frenzied activity of the weapons plant. They would have found adequate housing in Hot Springs, not just for single men but for whole families—and Gene had an entire house assigned to him. I imagine him walking to work to save money. I imagine him sitting in an office in his shirtsleeves. Maybe there's a Betty Grable calendar on the wall. I see Gene dipping the sharp nib of his pen in India ink and leaning into his drawing board. I've set this scene in the stifling heat of the Arkansas summer, so the windows are open, and a huge rotary fan is going overhead. I step closer and see that Gene and the other draftsmen are drawing bomb casings.

"Well, of course I remember Pearl Harbor," my mother says on my tape, the tone of her voice adding, *What do you think I am, an idiot?* She and my grandmother were working in the shop when they heard on the radio that the Japanese had bombed Pearl Harbor. She was five months pregnant with me. It was a Sunday. They'd never heard of Pearl Harbor. "It was out around Hawaii, in that part of the world, I guess. They sent our boys to Hawaii and then on and out into the Pacific, then people got concerned. But really, the war didn't touch little towns like Wheeling."

What on earth is she talking about? Of course the war touched little towns like Wheeling. It touched everybody. But that unfocused reaction to the war and her disclaimer of any involvement in it is typical of my mother—indicative of the distance she felt from nearly all of the great affairs of the world. One of the roles she had learned to play superbly well was that of the "dumb little thing"—as she

"As soon as the war started, they landed a fat government contract to build and operate the Pine Bluff facility sixty-three miles away. Magnesium and thermite incendiary bombs were manufactured, assembled, and stored at Pine Bluff. Some of the bombs used to torch Dresden might well have been manufactured there." U.S. Army photograph of the Pine Bluff Arsenal assembly line, ca. 1942, courtesy of the Encyclopedia of Arkansas History and Culture.

occasionally referred to herself. It would have been an easy role to pick up as a girl growing up in the Teens, as the baby in the family. "Dumb little things" aren't ever quite sure who is fighting whom, where, and for what purpose. Playing the dumb little thing would have appealed to men, would have appealed to Gene.

He probably thought of her as many men did of their wives—as "the little woman"—in my mother's case, an accurate description: she was four-foot-eleven. He probably liked it when *the little woman* played *the dumb little thing*; he would have seen her as cute and feminine. "Dictoral" she called him.

> I couldn't take his, "You do this, this way, no other way." I had worked since I was sixteen, and here I was in my thirties, and I wasn't about to have anyone tell me what to do. I knew I could make a living, and no way was I going to kow-tow to him. And he expected it. He was of the old, I guess, French background that he was the boss, the head of the house. But he ran into a snag when he married me.

Unlike most Americans, Gene would remember the last years of the Depression as not bad at all. He'd never been unemployed. He hadn't been making much money, but he'd always had enough. *If you watch your pennies, you can get by on next to nothing*, I imagine him trying to tell his wife. It didn't matter how hard the times were, you could always find a dollar here, and another one there, to put away in the bank. Any little extra you picked up for teaching or performing—well, it all added up. Ten pennies make a dime, and ten dimes make a dollar.

Folks in the Depression had needed brightening up, and Gene had done his best to oblige them. Every chance he got, he mounted the stage himself, as a singer, a comic, a tap dancer, a clown in blackface. Wheeling Steel had even paid him to stage shows—how lucky could a man get in the middle of a depression? But in Hot Springs, no one was paying him to stage shows. The Japanese had bombed Pearl Harbor, and there was a war on. There were no more shows to be staged and no more kids to be taught to dance. Things were serious, by God.

At forty-one, Gene's too old to be in the war, but he's doing war work, and he's proud of it. He and the other men in the engineering department follow the war the way American men always follow wars—exactly the way they follow baseball. They feel themselves to be a part of something far bigger than their individual lives. They share a sense of purpose, of dedication, that carries them day to day. They're doing men's work. They're going to beat those goddamn sneaky Japs at their own game. But then Gene comes home from that comradely, masculine, *satisfying* environment to find a wife who doesn't give a damn about the war. He's dog tired, trapped with a moody woman who can't see any farther than the walls of the house where she's living—who can't talk about anything but *the baby*.

I had been born prematurely, had always been underweight, had never lived up to the expectations on the doctors' charts, but it was in Hot Springs where I really started to go downhill. I might have been suffering from what we'd now call "failure to thrive syndrome," but then they just called me "sickly." I was supposed to be eating soft baby foods, but anything my mother fed me flowed straight through me. Instead of gaining weight, I was losing it. She was worried to death. She must have been afraid that I was on my way out.

I watched her all the time. I didn't sleep as much as other babies. Sometimes I cried just like other babies, but I also went for long periods when I didn't cry. Wherever I lay, I followed her with my eyes. I seemed to be watching everything.

My mother had always been the baby in the family, but now she *had* a baby. She didn't have a clue what to do with a baby. My grandmother had made it seem so easy. She'd been there the day I was born. She would have been there, too, when I came home from the hospital. She would have shown my mother how to change diapers, how to give me a bottle, how to lay me down properly in my crib so I didn't suffocate in my sleep. As long as my mother had been in Wheeling, she could have picked up the phone and there, on the other end of the line, would have been her reliable, helpful, comforting mother, who knew everything there was to know about babies. But now my mother was in Hot Springs, and it might as well have been out around Hawaii along with Pearl Harbor—that's how far away it felt. She wrote to her mother every day, but it took a week to get an answer back, and, good Lord, in a week, the baby could have died.

Alone with a baby. Every minute feels like an hour. What if he *is* dying? My mother believes the same thing that Gene believes—that everyone believes—that every woman knows how to be a mother. She looks inside herself and can't find anything telling her how to be a mother. She doesn't know what to do. There's no one to ask. She's desperately afraid. What if she's the worst thing a woman could possibly be—a bad mother?

One afternoon when I was taking a nap, my mother stepped into the room to see how I was doing and saw a scorpion in my crib. I was asleep. The scorpion was not more than an inch from my cheek. My mother could never tell this story without a shudder of horror and revulsion passing visibly through her entire body. In my recorded account, she runs out of words and utters a chilling high-pitched wail. The damned thing must have been, as I discover now, a striped bark scorpion, common to Arkansas. It would have been attracted to the moisture of my breath. An adult would have been about two-and-a-half-inches long with a tail of a particularly nasty, putrescent yellow—except for the stinger, which would have been dark brown or black. My mother did not know the name of the scorpion. There are no scorpions in Wheeling, West Virginia. She had never seen a scorpion in her life.

The sting of the striped bark scorpion is hardly ever lethal, but my mother did not know that. I was an underweight infant, and maybe it could have killed me. My mother was utterly certain that it would kill me. As horrified and repulsed as she was, there was only one thing she could do, and she did it instinctively and instantly. She slapped the scorpion with the back of her hand and knocked it across the room. Then she grabbed me up from my crib, settled me safely on the couch in the living room, and hurried back to look for the scorpion. She knew she had to kill it. She stripped the bedding out of the crib and shook it. She looked behind drapes and under blinds and in dark corners and in the back of the closet. She went through every inch of that room. She didn't leave a single object unturned. She never found the scorpion.

No one could accuse Gene of being a bad provider. He was doing his best for his family. "I need some help," my mother had said, so he'd hired a local woman. Neither "mammy" nor "maid" were words my mother ever used; my mother called her, simply, "the help." In my mother's stories "the help" is as much of a stereotype as anything from a '40s movie—a culturally constructed image so seamless and opaque that I can't see behind it.

"I'd look out the window," my mother told me, "and here comes this big black

"Unlike most Americans, Gene (here, in 1938) would remember the last years of the Depression as not bad at all. He hadn't been making much money, but he'd always had enough. Any little extra you picked up for teaching or performing — well, it all added up. Folks in the Depression had needed brightening up, and Gene had done his best to oblige them. Every chance he got, he mounted the stage himself." All family photographs courtesy of the author.

lady." She wore high, black lace-up shoes and carried a black umbrella to ward off the summer sun. She walked to my parents' house every morning, folded the umbrella, leaned it against the wall on the porch, unlaced her shoes, took them off, arranged them neatly by the umbrella, and worked the entire day barefoot. As soon as she stepped into the house, she got out the flour and baked a batch of biscuits. She baked biscuits for breakfast, lunch, and dinner. My mother would say, "That's very nice, thank you. But, please, don't bake any more biscuits."

"Yes'm," the help said. In my mother's reports, that's the main thing she said. My mother's instructions had no effect whatsoever. The biscuits continued to appear for breakfast, lunch, and dinner. My mother threw out biscuits by the dozen. My mother hated biscuits for the rest of her life. When I was growing up, I never even *saw* a biscuit until I was in high school and eating dinner at a friend's.

Doctors in the '40s believed that babies should be trained to fit into a predetermined schedule. The doctor who'd delivered me in Wheeling had given my mother just such a schedule, and she was doing her best. The help knew better. She held me constantly. She rocked me and never put me down. My mother would say, "Don't do that. Put him in his crib."

"Yes'm," the help would say. She'd put me in my crib. My mother would go in the other room. When my mother came back, the black lady would always have picked me up again.

My mother would have known nothing about the help. She would never have attempted a conversation with her. By the time she told me the stories, she'd forgotten her name. From the experiences of a lifetime in Hot Springs, Arkansas, the help would have learned to play dumb even better than my mother, but I imagine her going home at night, saying to her husband, or her own kids, "That white lady don't know the first thing about babies." When a baby cries, you pick it up.

Help or no help, my mother was desperate. She had to talk to somebody. She heard from some of the other wives about an old doctor they all swore by, a pediatrician, so she went to see him. She had me in a diaper, and a t-shirt, and a romper, and shoes and socks, and a sweater. She'd even wrapped me in a blanket. The doctor was a large, dignified man with a head of thick snow-white hair. He spoke as everyone did—in that slow southern drawl that grated on my mother's nerves. In no time flat he had me stripped down to the buff. He poked at the front of me with his finger, turned me over and poked at my back. "Mrs. Maillard," he said, "you've got too much clothes on this baby. It's the middle of the summer, for heaven's sake. *Never* put that many clothes on him. Don't put anything on him but a diaper."

My mother always laughed when she told this story—laughing at herself, at the dumb little thing she had been—but at the time, it wasn't the least bit funny. "Take him home and give him mashed bananas," the doctor told her. "Feed him as much as he can eat all day long."

Anywhere, Arkansas—your backwoods cracker existence is over. Every able-bodied male between the ages of eighteen and thirty has been sucked out of the population. The big bucks have arrived, courtesy of the U.S. Government. Every able-bodied female has a job if she wants one, but she's got to leave home to get it. Farms are abandoned. Kids are left behind. Appalled, the older folks are writing letters to the editor. The war has brought a "boom in badness," they're saying. Prostitutes are piling up in the hotel rooms in Little Rock. Women with honest jobs are strutting around town in high heels and slacks. Underage boys are roaming the state in gangs, making a nuisance of themselves, breaking into folks' homes. Worst of all are the teenage "victory girls" who are doing their patriotic best to "improve the morale" of our boys in uniform—and picking up a little hard cash for their efforts. The rates of syphilis and gonorrhea are skyrocketing—my God, it's an epidemic! The authorities in Hot Springs do what everybody else in the state is jawing about but nobody else has the guts to do. They impose a curfew to keep those damnable teenagers off the street at night.

Trains are rolling into Hot Springs at all hours, dumping sick and wounded servicemen, carrying away the ones who've recovered. The Army has already taken over the immense Eastman Hotel, is in the process of gobbling up the smaller hotels on Bathhouse Row. None of the hustling, overheated, jammed up, chaotic human mess of Hot Springs has carried over into my mother's stories, but that alien world must have pressed in on her from all sides. She's trying to buy bananas. I will set this scene in the farmers' market I remember from my childhood—a long barn of a building with stalls running along both walls. My mother, pushing me in a carriage, has to maneuver through a million damned strangers. She's staring into stall after stall of fruit and vegetables. She can't find a single banana.

A tune that had been all the rage the year my mother was twelve must surely have been rattling in her brain— *YES, we have no bananas!* Corn, beans, potatoes, carrots, tomatoes, lettuce, even rutabagas—but no bananas. Apples, berries, melons, maybe even oranges from Florida—but no bananas. Hot Springs is a demonic puzzle, a hell hole that breeds scorpions but no bananas. She'd searched for the scorpion for hours. Her baby is dying, and she can't find bananas. Defeated, she goes back to the doctor. He laughs at her. "The bananas you're used to—those long yella things?—that's not the way they are down here. Our bananas are short and green."

My mother mashed the short, green, stubby, alien bananas and fed them to me. When she couldn't take any more bananas or any more baby, she told the help to feed them to me. The effect was immediate. My body must have been crying out for starch and potassium. I gained weight. I slept through the night. Gene complained about the doctor's bill. "He told you to feed him bananas?" I imagine him saying. "That's what I'm paying for? And I'm paying him again because he had to tell you what they look like? Good Lord, Aileen, where's your common sense?"

"My mother believes the same thing that Gene believes — that everyone believes — that every woman knows how to be a mother. She looks inside herself and can't find anything telling her how to be a mother. She doesn't know what to do. There's no one to ask. She's desperately afraid. What if she's the worst thing a woman could possibly be — a bad mother?" Mother and son, 1942.

"Gene and I used to walk downtown," my mother told me, "not to buy, no, to *look*. And anything that I needed, like a pair of shoes for you, we had to go to four different places, price them, look at the material, what they were made of, see if they were any good, then go home and compare, and then buy the best value. I never could go anyplace and buy it right now, and that drove me crazy. I was used to my own money, to going downtown. If I liked that, I bought it, no questions asked; it was *my* money. But not with Gene Maillard."

Many couples argue themselves into a single fight around which everything else revolves, a fight they keep having over and over again. If my parents had a fight like that, it was surely about *the money*. When it came to *the money*, my parents didn't merely have a difference of opinion; they had bitterly opposed worldviews. "Gene thought I was the most extravagant person he ever saw," my mother told me, shaking her head in amazement that anyone could think that of her.

There were things from steaks to television sets that we simply couldn't afford. We didn't think about "such foolishness," as my grandmother put it. What on earth could Gene have objected to about my mother? It couldn't have been any particular extravagant purchase. It must have been her attitude. He would have sensed instantly that she didn't think the way he did.

To my mother, money was filthy lucre. Disreputable and slimy, it was both absolutely necessary and absolutely disgusting. She would have preferred to live in a world in which someone else handled the money (a man, of course), where it was never discussed. Only the lowest of the low would mention money. When an exact figure came out of anyone's mouth—the twenty-five dollars for a suit or five thousand dollars for a house—you knew immediately that such a person was far down on the social ladder, beneath your contempt. Money was supposed to mysteriously appear and take care of things—although we know that it doesn't, and so did my mother. She never had money in the bank; she had debts. The money is what got her out of bed every morning and sent her off to do the work she hated.

But she always had her impulsive moments. She could suddenly decide that we were going out to dinner and then to a show, which we couldn't really afford—because sometimes you just had to do things like that or life wasn't worth living. When she was old, she was a sucker for weird gadgets advertised on television, would buy them on impulse and send them to me—a specially lined ice tray that popped out cubes at a touch, huge steel nails you drove though potatoes to make them bake faster.

How did the money get to be so powerful and disgusting? The money was what could have sent her to college and given her an entirely different life, but didn't, because the father she adored—openhanded and generous and carefree, as always—threw it away in a poker game. That was both the upside and downside, the angel and the demon of a man. A man could piss the money away, or he could spend it lavishly on you. If Gene had wanted to keep her, he should have

"Trains are rolling into Hot Springs at all hours, dumping sick and wounded servicemen, carrying away the ones who've recovered. The Army has already taken over the immense Eastman Hotel, is in the process of gobbling up the smaller hotels on Bathhouse Row." Bathhouse Row, Hot Springs, Arkansas, ca. 1905, courtesy of the Collections of the Library of Congress.

lavished his money on her. If he'd been able to do that, she might well have been at his bedside when he died at nearly ninety-six. But he was no more capable of lavishing his money on her than she was of saving the milk in the cereal bowl to use the next morning.

Gene's view of money was entirely different. In Gene's mind, money was life itself. It was the difference between eating and not eating, going to school and not going to school, making something of yourself or being stuck in poverty your whole life, chasing one job or another from pillar to post like a glassblower. If money is life, then the worth of your life can be directly measured by the amount of money you've got in the bank. If you carry this notion to its logical extreme, then the money in the bank is not something that you would want to spend—it's the way to keep score.

Gene would have known that my mother was not playing his game and had no interest in learning to play it. He would have lied to her automatically, made himself out to be poorer than he was. He would never have allowed her to see his financial records. She was a trained and efficient bookkeeper, and there's no way she would have missed the little hoard that was already starting to pile up in the bank.

They're out one afternoon, pushing me in the baby carriage, not shopping but looking, and here comes the famous story of the nickel for a Coke. "Go home and drink water. It's free," he says. To deliver that line, you have to be pissed off—and not just about the nickel. You have to have been pissed off for so long that the nickel is the goddamned last straw—the latest beat in the ancient, interminable, irresolvable, and utterly maddening *fight*.

That's one way to play it. Here's another: Yes, he is angry, but he's trying to make a joke of it. "Come on, Aileen," he says with a laugh and a grin, "Go home and drink water. It's free." The joke's on her, on her extravagant ways, but it's on him too, an admission that he is—well, maybe just a little bit too tight with his money. How could she not get the joke? Nobody could say something like that and mean it.

No, that doesn't feel right. Okay, let me try it another way. Maybe he is trying it as a joke, delivers his line with a laugh, but it turns out to be one of those jokes we make all the time without understanding what we're doing—a joke that isn't really a joke, a joke with a stinger attached. The moment it's out of his mouth, he realizes how it must have sounded. He's appalled at himself but can't think of a damn thing to say that might fix it.

But no, I can't believe that version either. It wasn't a joke. I've finally caught up to him. I know him well enough by now to feel the fire of his outrage—to feel it burn in me too. It's a hell of a lot bigger than the nickel for a Coke.

What does she know about it? Did she ever go without eating because there was nothing to eat? Did she ever have to walk the neighborhood with her stomach aching, so hungry she was ready to kill, humiliating herself, begging—*Excuse me, can I sweep your porch? Shovel your coal? Can I do anything?* He's doing his best to be a good husband, a good father, to provide for his family. If she was a good wife, she wouldn't just take it for granted and piss the money away. She'd help him, count the pennies right along with him. That's what a good wife does. That's what his mother used to do. The most important thing he has to teach his son is the value of money, and if she was a good mother, she'd understand that.

The nickel for a Coke—he's said it, and he can't take it back. Gene and Aileen can't do anything but keep on walking—in an oppressive silence so loaded with subtext that we, the audience, become acutely aware of the squeaky wheels of the baby carriage. The camera dollies back slowly to give us a longer and longer shot—as the doomed couple is lost among the crowd of shoppers on that Saturday afternoon in 1942 in Hot Springs, Arkansas.

If my mother's official statement about the end of their marriage blamed *the money*, Gene's official statement—his summary worked out years later—blamed my grandmother, or, as he put it, *the mother-in-law*, a standard butt of jokes in those days. If a comedian opened his monologues with the line, "Well, the mother-in-law dropped in the other day . . . ," the audience would start to chuckle, sure there was a good story coming. In Gene's accounts, my grandmother is always standing in the background, one hefty arm upraised, clutching, not a rolling pin, as a cartoon mother-in-law would, but a carving knife. That was the demonic figure that Gene presented to his friends and Masonic brothers, the reason his marriage failed, and there's a grain of truth to it.

Except for the three years when she was married to Gene, my mother lived with her mother her entire life. Hot Springs was not merely strange, alien, incomprehensible, and scorpion-ridden; it was far from her mother. She wrote to her mother every day and expected a letter back every day. If she didn't get one, she'd call her long distance, running up Gene's phone bill. My mother was *alone with a baby* and needed all the help she could get from the only person who could give it to her. She also felt guilty—as though she'd abandoned her mother: "I worried about her not having enough. I'd been with her all my life, and I knew she was staying up until midnight trying . . . putting that last stitch in something to earn a dollar, and I just couldn't stand it." Gene may never have voiced the question, "Do you want to live with your mother or do you want to live with me?" but it must have been playing constantly in his mind.

It seems sad to me that the black lady who helped out my mother has lost her name but a walk-on character with one line of dialogue has retained hers. A young couple was living across the street from my parents. The wife's maiden name had been Schellenberg, so her nickname was Shelly. "If her husband said jump, she jumped three times," my mother told me. "I don't know whether all southern girls are like that or not. They were back then. The man ruled the roost. But I'd worked too long for that. Hum."

Shelly Fraser said to my mother, "You know what's wrong with your marriage? Your husband's more in love with you than you are with him."

If that was Shelly's invitation to girl talk, my mother wasn't having any. "That's none of your business," she snapped at her.

Shelly must have hit a nerve. My mother was feeling that sickening, claustrophobic, trapped sense of guilt we get when people love us more than we love

"Except for the three years when she was married to Gene, my mother lived with her mother her entire life. Hot Springs was not merely strange, alien, incomprehensible, and scorpion-ridden; it was far from her mother. She wrote to her mother every day and expected a letter back every day. If she didn't get one, she'd call her long distance, running up Gene's phone bill. My mother was alone with a baby and needed all the help she could get from the only person who could give it to her." Mother and daughter, ca. 1923.

them. She couldn't always have hated Gene Maillard's guts; at times she must have thought, *Oh, poor Gene*. She wanted to retain something of her independence, but she also wanted to be a good wife. As everybody knew then, a man has needs and a good wife satisfies her husband's needs.

I imagine Gene looking at his wife and thinking, *Oh, my God, why her?* He'd never had trouble getting girls; he could have married almost anyone else, but he'd chosen Aileen, and he was still trying to make the marriage work with her. He doesn't know why, but he loves her—and she's the mother of his son, and he wants a family. I imagine them in bed—his desperation. She puts up with him because that's what a good wife does. But he keeps asking something of her with his body—*Look at me, make me the center of your life. I'm your husband. Love me*. Night after night it gets more mechanical and desperate. She's drifting farther and farther away. He can feel her going.

The things that we know deep in our bones, with every fiber of our being—the things that our entire life and experience have trained us to know—carry an absolute conviction. Knowing those things is like knowing that we have to fight our way straight to the surface for air.

Gene knows, at that deep level, that we can be moved unexpectedly from town to town, that people in our lives can come and go, that even the people we love can be here one day and gone the next, but in the midst of that terrible flux and uncertainly, there's one thing that's stable, one thing we can always trust, and that's the money.

My mother knows, at that same deep level, that there is only one person she can trust, the one person who's been there forever, the one person who's never let her down and never will: her mother. She also knows that any man she loves will betray her, and when he does, it will be about the money.

Were my parents living in Hot Springs together only a few months or for as long as a year? How old was I, exactly, when she left him? I was wearing shoes—my mother and Gene had shopped for them—but you can put shoes on a baby before he can walk. My mother's stories have only one season attached to them—the oppressive heat of the Arkansas summer. At the height of the summer, I would have been six months old. When we boarded the train that would carry us away from there, I was old enough to eat mashed bananas but still drinking formula from a bottle. Did she leave him before my first birthday or after it? Exact dates might matter to me, trying to write about it, but they don't matter to my mother. For her, Hot Springs is a mythic time that lasts longer than anything that can be measured on a calendar. Hot Springs will always be there, as big as it needs to be, recreating itself continually in an eternal present—until dementia eats up her memory.

The bananas have done the trick. I am eating. I'm getting bigger. She can see the pink coming into my cheeks. I'm sleeping better. But she's traded places with

"'If her husband said jump, she jumped three times,' said my mother (here, in her graduation photo, 1929). 'I don't know whether all southern girls are like that or not. They were back then. The man ruled the roost. But I'd worked too long for that. Hum.'"

me. The blazing summer sun turns the house into a fetid steambath. It reeks of baby shit, ammonia from the diaper pail, and alien mashed bananas. The stench makes her sick. There's nowhere she can go to get away from it, because she can't leave the baby. She keeps throwing away plate after plate of biscuits—and that might be funny someday, but it's not funny now. She can't eat anything. She can't keep anything down. She can't even imagine anything she might want to eat. She's losing weight. She can't sleep. Any pillow or blanket or shadow might have a scorpion under it.

My mother has no support. Her mother and her sister are far away. Shelly across the street has tried to include her in the wives' network, but my mother—proud, private, stubborn—shut her down. My mother knows that she can't keep running back to the doctor—Gene would have a fit. The one person in her life who understands babies is arriving every morning, taking off her shoes and walking in barefoot, but it would never occur to my mother to talk to her.

My mother gets up in the night and cleans the house again. She looks in every dark corner, pokes into the back of every cupboard and closet. This doesn't have any words. She can feel it in her stomach all the time. It never lets up. She can't think straight, and it scares her to death.

"There's a war on," Gene says. She knows that. Who does he think she is? She can't talk to Mother, tell her how bad it is. She says to herself that she doesn't want to worry her, but it's more than that. Keith may be doing okay for now, but for how long? What if he gets sick again? What if she doesn't put him down right and he dies in his sleep? What if *anything*? She can't take her eyes off the baby for a minute, and she can't talk to Gene. He's *a man*, what would he know? If the measure of a man is his money in the bank, the measure of a woman is how well she does as a mother. Everybody knows that motherly instincts are something you're born with, so she knows she's a failure. She can't admit that to anyone, not now and not ever.

One day, when Gene's at work, she calls her sister, Martha. She finds the only words she will ever be able to say about Hot Springs: "I can't live like this."

"Well, for Pete's sake, Aileen, you don't have to live like that. You'll come to my house. I'll get you and Keith back on your feet, and then I'll drive you to Wheeling."

Many pieces of this story I heard so many times that they became worn smooth as old banisters. The black lady is holding me on her lap, rocking me. Big tears are rolling down her cheeks. "Oh, please," she says, "don't take my baby away from me."

How it ended was something I heard only once. I'm certain that my mother had no intention of telling me, but every day while I was interviewing her, I pointed her in that direction. I did it as methodically and coldly as a cop interrogating a witness. At the end of the fourth day her unquenchable anger thrust her back nearly sixty years, right into the heart of it. "Well, Gene, I'm leaving you," she said to him.

I have to set the scene somewhere, so I'll put them in the kitchen. It's night, and the help has gone home. I'm asleep in my crib. My mother's sitting in a kitchen chair. As I imagine it, Gene, who never raised his voice, gets even quieter. "I can't live like this," she's saying to him. "I wasn't raised like this."

"'I worried about her not having enough. I'd been with her all my life, and I knew she was staying up until midnight trying . . . putting that last stitch in something to earn a dollar, and I just couldn't stand it.'" The author's grandmother, Mabel Sharp, ca. 1950.

In the scene I'm writing, my father has just stood up. To distance himself, he's leaning against the wall. To hold himself in, he's folded his arms across his chest. He's heard her say things like that before, so his first impulse is to make a joke of it, but then he guesses that would be crazy, so he stops himself. She's mad as a hornet, and everything he says, or tries to say, just makes matters worse. He's been watching this go on for a long time now. It's almost as bad as standing by, helplessly, and watching his father, and then his mother, die. Maybe he says, *Come on, Aileen, tomorrow's another day.* A crushing hopelessness settles onto him. Nothing he says is ever right.

I've seen my mother in a fury. Her huge blue eyes freeze into a rigid stare. Her voice goes as bitter as vinegar. She makes a small smacking sound with her lips—a nasty click—rolls her eyes up at the ceiling. She focuses on my father's eyes. Now that she's leaving him, taking the baby home to her mother, she's not afraid—not even slightly. She doesn't have to take any more of his crap. Everything civil, gentle, domesticated about her drops away. All that's left is the icy clarity of her outrage.

Gene can't stand looking at her. He turns away, searches for words. When he speaks, his voice is so stifled he can barely hear himself. Maybe he says, *We'll get through this, Aileen.* Maybe he says, *It's rough on everybody. There's a war on.*

It's driving her up the wall—Gene's quiet, his control, and then his *silence.* How can he just stand there like that, the dictoral son of a bitch? He's patronizing her again, treating her like the little woman again. Doesn't he get it? She has to make sure that he gets it. She fires another burst at him, but he's taking it all just as calm as a lake. She can hear her own voice—loud, emphatic, dripping with sarcasm—and she lets the seductive power of it carry her. Everything she says is meant to cut to the quick.

Gene is beginning to get it. He's baffled, at the end of his rope. She's not kidding this time. She's made plans. She's got it all worked out. She's *got the money.* She's talked to her sister, talked to her *goddamned mother.* Long distance. God knows what those calls must have cost.

She's pushed him right to the limit. He's compromised and compromised and done his best, but he's gone as far as he can, and he's not going to give another inch. She went and named the baby Keith when he was working out of town— pure spite. He's thinking of his father now. Sometimes when he's drifting off to sleep, he can still hear Papa's breath rasping in that back bedroom. *My son was supposed to be named Eugene. To honor Papa. My God, Aileen doesn't understand a damned thing.*

Now I don't have to imagine what they said because this is what she told me. When I first heard it, I imagined them yelling at each other, but now, having written my way here, I don't think so. Gene finds his voice again. It's clear and hard, but he's not yelling. "You'll never get a penny."

My mother's not yelling either. She's simply stating the facts, the way it's going to be, now and forever. "You'll never know him."

That trip back from Hot Springs—It was a troop train. They were transporting troops. I was lucky to get on that train. They had one car with seats, train seats in it, and it was like a special car. You had to pay twice as much for the fare, and they gave me a little compartment of a bed and a toilet in this little room that wasn't any bigger than right here. And that's where I was, but no food. You were hungry, and you started to cry. They moved the train onto a side track so this long troop train could go past, and there we sat, and we were supposed to get into Cincinnati hours before. And there we sat. And sat. And you were hungry, and you started screaming.

They were all sitting on the floor. All these fellas. With their backs up against each other and their legs—But anyhow, and this tall southern fella, a soldier, knocked on the door, and he says, "Is your baby hungry?"

I said, "Yes."

He says, "I have two of my own." He says, "Bring him"—or, "Give him to me." He reached down, and he picked you up, and he took my hand, and he says, "Catch ahold of my belt and don't let go."

He went through that troop train—I was right behind him—to the kitchen, and he says, "We need some milk."

The chef, or the man in charge, says, "Nope. Nobody gets milk."

He says, "I want some milk for this baby!"

And the man turned around—looked at him, looked at you, and he gave it. And you had been on a dumb formula all your life. You didn't drink cow's milk. But that's what he gave us, and that's what I gave you, and you drank it. Oh, dear.

Martha and Harley met me in Cincinnati, and they had waited hours. They kept saying that it'll be here so and so and so. And they waited for the train to come in. I remember seeing Martha. I had you, and you were—I was exhausted. All I did when I got off the train was take you and hand you to Martha. I don't remember much from then on. Harley caught ahold of me and got me through the—wherever we were—to the car, and I just passed out. I handed you to Martha, and Harley put his arm around me, and I don't remember anything else till I got awake in College Corner in bed.

Martha was appalled. She called Mother. I remember hearing her. Says, "Well, we got her. And she's here. And I'm going to keep her for two or three weeks," and Mother must have asked why, and Martha says, "Well, she's tired." She didn't go into it. But I had lost so much weight because I couldn't eat. Martha was mighty good to me—and Harley. He was putting the money out. I was in bed two weeks out at Martha's. And she took care of you. The doctor— he was a friend of theirs—he says, "Just let her sleep. If she gets awake, give her some soup." Lord, Keith, I only weighed seventy-nine pounds.

I could end this story with my mother lying in bed at Martha's, watching the light fade out at the window, as she listens to Martha talking to my grandmother long distance, telling her, "Well, she's tired." I could imagine myself somewhere in Martha's house, crying or sleeping. But I've done that before, and this time I'm going to stay with Gene. I'd always known that my mother had been devastated by Hot Springs, but Gene was just as devastated. He's thinking, *Well, there she goes, Gene, with your son. Three strikes and you're out.*

The prose in the paragraph beginning "Anywhere, Arkansas" is mine. All of the information contained in that paragraph, however, comes from C. Calvin Smith's excellent book, War and Wartime Changes: The Transformation of Arkansas 1940–1945 *(The University of Arkansas Press, 1986).*

Catfish and Home

by Josh Eure

Baseball has long been a favorite pastime of small towns across America, but for Josh Eure's hometown of
Hertford, North Carolina, the sport took on legendary qualities after the town's own Jim "Catfish" Hunter
pitched for the Oakland A's and New York Yankees on his way to a Hall of Fame career. Near Mountain Home,
Arkansas, 1938, courtesy of the Collections of the Library of Congress.

was never much for baseball. It wasn't that I hated the sport. I simply had no skill for it. A pop-fly to my left field usually went uncaught—never mind my batting. I was tall, arms hung ape-like from my body, and my movements were too stretched out, languid flourishes that were useless. I wasn't built for it. But in Hertford, North Carolina, where baseball hung in every home, office, classroom, and service station, a boy like me had little else to choose from. Hertford *was* baseball.

Some would say our sleepy hometown fell in love with the game when America fell for Catfish in the 1960s and '70s. Jimmy "Catfish" Hunter, a local hero, pitched for the Oakland Athletics and the New York Yankees (helping them to three straight pennants), played in the World Series six times, made eight All-Star teams, won 224 games, and in 1987 was inducted into the Baseball Hall of Fame— all the while maintaining his small-town farming roots: his Hertford roots. His professional career spanned 1965 to 1979, and in that time, he became Hertford's Prometheus, our link to the gods. He played every game with the shotgun pellets from a childhood hunting accident lodged in his foot, the result of winter mornings in the woods, doe-urine-splashed boots from stalking prey until nightfall, and natives imagined he held a major piece of them in his cleats. When he came back home for good at the age of thirty-three, he was royalty. The winner of the Cy Young Award, pitcher of a perfect game in '68, the subject of a Bob Dylan song, a titan in our town. Because of Catfish, Hertford had a name. It would be remembered.

Hertford did have its own appeal, most of which was lost on me growing up. It's a simple town. It still retains a kind of calm, a repose all too swiftly fading (yet still lingering on southern back roads). It's one of the first permanent settlements in North Carolina, dating to the late 1600s, and home to one of the oldest buildings in the state: the Newbold-White House. Impressive Victorian and Georgian homes still mark the road winding along the Perquimans River. Tall, pillared structures framed by magnolias or weeping willows. Adorned in Spanish moss, cypress trees, melancholy and stoic, stand in the shallow water, osprey nesting in their limbs. An old 1950s-style malt shop thrives downtown. Dogbox-equipped flatbeds line the shoulders of various side roads, as hunters discuss the goings-on of whatever game is in season. There's racial tension, to be sure, but it simmers quietly—the surface somehow mostly still. The air practically carries southern ease, a cliché aura of small-town familiarity, as people meet and greet with smiles and *how do*'s comfortable in their everyday routine.

And that might've been image enough, but legislators and local business owners wanted to parade Hertford's quality. What would Hertford be without Catfish? A great mural now greets all who drive through downtown, homage to various aspects of our town's history and so-called progress. There is, of course, a

"A great mural now greets all who drive through downtown. There is, of course, a giant Yankees cap with a ball poised before it in the very center of the painted wall, a peculiar icon for a small, southern town if you don't know its history. Beside it stands a Civil War soldier saluting an imposing Confederate flag, the source of much debate today. A silhouette of two Pilgrim settlers in the foreground, and to the left a Native American perches on a cliff above the river, watching two boys play in metal buckets." Photograph courtesy of John Eure.

giant Yankees cap with a ball poised before it in the very center of the painted wall, a peculiar icon for a small, southern town if you don't know its history. Beside it stands a Civil War soldier saluting an imposing Confederate flag, the source of much debate today. A silhouette of two Pilgrim settlers in the foreground, and to the left a Native American perches on a cliff above the river, watching two boys play in metal buckets. From that river a famous log juts forth with three turtles sunning lazily atop it. A tacky and, to some, offensive masterpiece, no doubt, but it remains endearing to most locals—evidence of context for a hero, proof the town exists.

We would see Hertford's hero around town at times—in the pharmacy, at the Hertford Café or local ball games—and he was usually pleasant. Catfish would smile and wave if he knew us, or simply tip his hat. But we'd also heard tales, rumors like newspaper headlines. "Catfish Fights with Parent at Soccer Game." Scandals were big news, of course, but they only served to validate him as truly one of us—or them. To me, Hertford was a family I didn't belong to. I'd been adopted at thirteen by a local man, and if you looked closely, the difference was plain. I was only a witness to the town, a watchful refugee.

I played Little League, because *everyone* did. The community hung on those games. Parents were usually frenzied by the final innings, as were the coaches, Catfish among them, and his presence undoubtedly played a role in the league's significance. We worked for him. Dust filled the dry evenings as freckle-faced kids ground cleats into the sport that gave their hometown meaning. Big League Chew filled near every cheek, and younger boys and girls flitted about, mimicking players on teams they one day hoped to join. Even bench riders felt the distinction of those hard-earned plays, dugouts as alive as the bleachers. The town fell on each pitch, cried for each run scored. And it was the same for every baseball league up through varsity. Even I felt it.

I'd struck out twice already one game, and with slicked palms, heaving a weighted Easton bat from side to side, I had no hope for better. I tried to chock the weights off by driving the bat to the ground, firm and confident, but I shook with the force. It took two tries. I approached the plate, watching a teammate march to first, bow-legged, and I prayed to be walked, too. Legs vibrating as I scuffed my cleats in the dirt, back and forth, bending my knees, bouncing, lifting the bat from my shoulder. I tried to look like other players, cool, ready.

Catfish stood by the other team's dugout, his face shadowed by the brim of his hat. I couldn't see his expression, but I knew he was watching me. I turned back to the pitcher. I saw his shoulder snap when he let go of the ball, like a famous bird-wing, graceful and fierce. I swung for Catfish, although I was certain I would walk to the bench defeated once more. I knew this. But I felt that strange buzz of connection, a crack to shiver the bat. I searched the clouds for a sign, proof of triumph, and there it was—the ball sailing across the field, every head gazing upward, following my great hit. I hopped—even skipped—toward first base, afraid to look away. As I hit the bag I saw the boy in left field, watched as my ball fell, not a bomb but a dud, and the umpire screamed my fate. *Out!* I heard an eruption from behind me, people railing at my bad luck. I looked for Catfish, saw him walking off toward the concession stand with his hands in his pockets. Still I smiled. I struck out again the next inning, but already I was a hero. Like Catfish. I asked my teammates if they saw how close it was, how I'd almost hit a homer. They nodded, punched my arm, Coach ruffled the hat off my head. Then they forgot.

I imagine for those kids with talent, it was a great atmosphere to grow up in. But it was tedious for a daydreamer like me. The quiet, outfield gardener. I'd never be able to call baseball my own, never was the pride of a team, but I did grow fond of the sport. It was a great game to watch from the outside, where I was. To see the blond boy from Belvedere hit another homer. To see the parents make a fuss over him. To watch your assumed family force a smile after your expected strike-out. The hotdogs always tasted better after a game where you'd at least hit a foul ball. You hadn't whiffed, you'd tell yourself. And you'd vainly rail with the bravado of an insider at how the ball should have gone an inch more in such-and-such a

"Catfish stood by the other team's dugout, his face shadowed by the brim of his hat. I couldn't see his expression, but I knew he was watching me. I turned back to the pitcher. I saw his shoulder snap when he let go of the ball, like a famous bird-wing, graceful and fierce. I swung for Catfish, although I was certain I would walk to the bench defeated once more. I knew this." Hertford's diamond, the famous field of the author's youth, courtesy of John Eure.

direction. You'd hope that blond homerun hitter would laugh and say he'd been there before. It was the camaraderie you craved from your adopted town, from the center of Catfish's Hertford.

Hertford's hero died in 1999 after a fall on concrete steps, Lou Gehrig's disease having greatly diminished his mobility. It wasn't immediate—he later passed away in his home—but it felt like the sudden end of more than a man's life. The town exploded with mourners in black suits and dresses—and media—in a way that might have put Catfish off. Hertford looked ridiculous all dressed up, the hound-dog in a sweater, but we'd lost our champion. Catfish already had run a highlighter over the map, though, drenching our home—the forgettable mess he loved—in brilliant ink.

"Big Bone Lick," "Big Talk," and "Flush"

THREE POEMS BY ROBERT MORGAN

". . . the Indians said the peaks
were talking to each other in
the idiom that mountains use. . ."
Pilot Mountain, North Carolina, photographed by AnDrew McKenzie, 2003,
courtesy of a GNU Free Documentation License.

Big Bone Lick

At Big Bone Lick the first explorers
found skeletons of elephants they said,
found ribs of wooly mammoths, tusks.
They dug out teeth the size of bricks
and skulls of giant bison, beavers.
In salty mud licked bare by elk
and deer and buffalo and bears
for ten millennia, the bones
seemed wreckage from a mighty dream,
a graveyard from a golden age,
or killing ground of titans. Here
they saw the ruins of a world
survived by its diminutives,
where Eden once gave way and shrank
to just a regular promised land
to fit our deadly, human scale.

Big Talk

When mountains boomed and boomed again
returning echoes all along
the chain, the Indians said the peaks
were talking to each other in
the idiom that mountains use
across the mighty distances
with giant syllables and rests.
White hunters feared it might be guns
or even cannon natives had
somehow acquired to warn them from
the better hunting grounds and streams,
the blasts as loud as thunder on
the clearest days and coldest nights.
Geologists would later hold
the groans and barks inside the ridge
were shelves of massive, restless rock
that slipped or dropped far down within
the mountains' guts, a fracture or
a crashing at some fault as part

of the tectonic conversation
among the continents as old
as planet earth or starry birth,
the mutter of creation's work.

Flush

A common sight in graveyards in
the countryside's the sunken grave.
Though times may vary in each case
the average age for graves to cave
is roughly half a century.
To compensate old folks would curve
the dirt in mounds above the site.
But after several years the box
below gives way and heavy earth
subsides, to settle, crush the whole
container of remains, the dust
of the beloved, as clay unites
with clay. And what is seen above
in turf's a new depression near
the stone, a pool of absence filled
by rain or snow or blowing leaves
until the spot is flush again,
until the human is replaced,
with hill and wind and planet's curve.

About the Contributors

Peter S. Carmichael is the Robert C. Fluhrer Professor of History and the Director of the Civil War Institute at Gettysburg College. He is the author and editor of four books, including *The Last Generation: Young Virginians in Peace, War, and Reunion*, and is currently finishing a cultural history of the common Civil War soldier and a study of Confederate slaves titled *The War for the Common Soldier*, forthcoming from UNC Press.

Godfrey Cheshire is a film critic, journalist, and the writer director of *Moving Midway*, a documentary about his family's North Carolina plantation.

David P. Cline is the Associate Director of the Southern Oral History Program at the University of North Carolina at Chapel Hill. He is the author of *Creating Choice: A Community Responds to the Need for Abortion and Birth Control, 1961–1973* and is currently working on several projects concerned with the intersection between Christian faith and social activism.

Josh Eure won the Dell Award and the Brenda L. Smart Prize and was finalist for *Glimmer Train*'s Short Story Award for New Writers. He also was nominated for a Best of the Net Award, and his work has appeared in the *Raleigh Review* and *Dell* magazine online. He received his MFA in Creative Writing from North Carolina State University.

Danny Fulks is Professor Emeritus at Marshall University. He has written two collections of nonfiction essays for the Jesse Stuart Foundation (Ashland, Kentucky), *Tragedy On Greasy Ridge* and *Tick Ridge Faces the South*, and has published in the *MacGuffin*, *Timeline*, *Backwoods Home*, *Hearthstone*, *Goldenseal*, *Bluegrass Unlimited*, the *Elementary School Journal*, the *Educational Forum*, *Now and Then*, and the *Appalachian Journal*. He lives in Huntington, West Virginia.

Sally Greene is an independent scholar whose interests include the law, literature, and history of the American South. Her essays have appeared in the *Southern Quarterly*, the *Mississippi Quarterly*, the *Journal of Modern Literature*, and the *North Carolina Law Review*. She is Associate Director of the UNC Center for the Study of the American South.

Keith Maillard was born and raised in West Virginia. Currently the Chair of the Creative Writing Program at the University of British Columbia, he is the author of thirteen novels and one poetry collection. "Hot Springs" is based upon a chapter from his forthcoming memoir, *Fatherless*.

Robert Morgan is a poet, novelist, and biographer. His most recent book is *Boone: A Biography* (2007), winner of the Kentucky Literary Award and finalist for the *Los Angeles Times* Book Award. He is the recipient of fellowships and awards from the Guggenheim and Rockefeller Foundations, the National Endowment for the Arts, and the American Academy of Arts and Letters, as well as an honorary degree from his alma mater, the University of North Carolina at Chapel Hill. Since 1971 he has taught at Cornell University, where he is now Kappa Alpha Professor of English.

Jessica Wilkerson is a doctoral candidate in Women's and Gender History at the University of North Carolina at Chapel Hill. Her research explores women's activism in the Mountain South in the 1970s. She is currently working with the Southern Oral History Program on the women's movement phase of their ongoing Long Civil Rights Movement research.

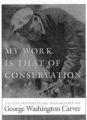

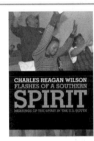
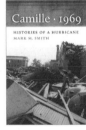
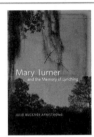
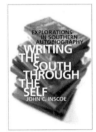

American Studies

with **American Studies International**

American Studies is a quarterly interdisciplinary journal sponsored by the Mid-America American Studies Association, the University of Kansas, and the Hall Center for the Humanities. With an editorial staff from a number of areas of study, the journal offers provocative perspectives on a variety of issues. Frequent special sections and special issues create a space for a broad discussion on a single topic. Articles on pedagogy inform the American Studies classroom. The book review section aims at keeping readers conversant with contemporary scholarship. *American Studies* first appeared in 1959, and has 1,000 current subscribers. In 2005 it merged with *American Studies International*, and welcomes submissions with an international perspective.

AARON DOUGLA/
AND THE
HARLEM RENAI//ANCE
William J. Harris, Special Editor

William J. Harris, "Introduction"

Gerald Early, "The New Negro Era and the Great African American Transformation"

Robert G. O'Meally, "The Flat Plane, The Jagged Edge: Aaron Douglas's Musical Art"

Terry Adkins, "The Vigilant Torch of an Olympian Painter"

Farah Jasmine Griffin, "On Time, In Time, Through Time: Aaron Douglas, *FIRE!!* and the Writers of the Harlem Renaissance"

David Krasner, "Dark Tower and the Saturday Nighters: Salons as Themes in African American Drama"

Amy Helene Kirschke, "The Burden of Black Womanhood: Aaron Douglas and the 'Apogée of Beauty'"

Richard J. Powell, "Paint that Thing! Aaron Douglas's Call to Modernism"

Stephanie Fox Knappe, *"Aaron Douglas: African American Modernist:* The Exhibition, the Artist, and His Legacy"

Cheryl R. Ragar, "The Douglas Legacy"

Special Price: $12 (domestic postage paid; add $10 for addresses outside of the U.S.)

— — — — — — — — — — — — — — — — — — — —

Fill out form and send check to:

Managing Editor
American Studies
1440 Jayhawk Blvd, Bailey 213
University of Kansas
Lawrence, KS 66045-7545

American Studies Journal 49:1/2 _____ @$12 _____

International shipping
(add $10.00 per volume) _____

Total: _____

Coming in 2011

journal
of
social
history

The *Journal of Social History* continues to define new areas of historical coverage and to clarify major interpretive issues in the field, with groupings of article on such subjects as the following:

Key Topics in Social History

-Emotions and humor
-Popular culture
-Poverty and crime
-Leisure and tourism
-Consumerism as a global topic
-Family and childhood
-Science and social history
-Material culture

-New approaches to race
  and slavery
-Urban history
-Sexuality and reproduction
-Community and authority
-Health and wellness
-Protest and deviance
-Social welfare and education

Plus: Many other articles and reviews, as the *Journal of Social History* maintains its role as a major outlet for historical research

Annual subscription rates:

Institutions	$125.00
Individuals	$45.00
Students	$30.00

Send check or credit card information to:

Journal of Social History
George Mason University
4400 University Drive MS3A2
Fairfax, VA 22030-4444

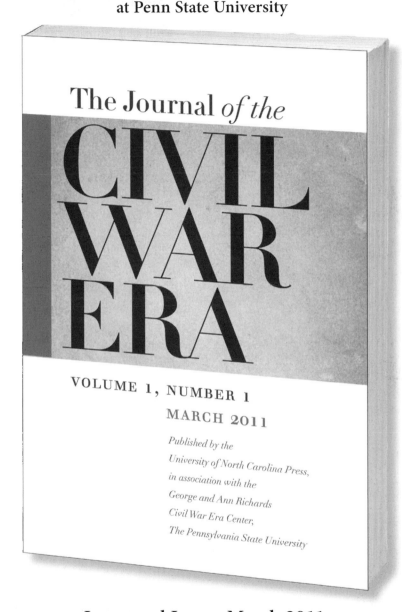

The Journal of Southern History
John B. Boles, *Editor*
Published quarterly by the Southern Historical Association

Annual membership in the Southern Historical Association includes four issues of the *Journal of Southern History* and a copy of the program for the annual meeting.

APPLICATION FOR MEMBERSHIP

Detach and mail with remittance to:
The Southern Historical Association
History Department, University of Georgia
Athens, Georgia 30602-1602

MEMBERSHIP CLASSES

☐ **Annual**   **$40.00**
☐ **Sustaining**   **$50.00**
☐ **Five-year**   **$160.00**
☐ **Enrolled Student**   **$10.00** (send certification)
☐ **Family Membership**   **$50.00** (includes two copies of the program for the annual meeting)
☐ **Life Membership**   **$600.00** (payable in quarterly installments within a year)
☐ **Retired**   **$25.00** (an active member of fifteen years or more, retiring for age, may request transfer to retired membership)
☐ **Institution**   **$60.00**

NOTICE: By action of the Executive Council, all memberships are on a calendar-year basis. Add $6.00 per year for foreign postage.

I enclose $_____ to pay for my dues in the Southern Historical Association.

Name _____

Address _____

E-mail address_____

Applications for student membership must be accompanied by this certificate signed by a faculty representative of the institution in which the applicant is currently enrolled.

I hereby certify that the person whose name appears on this application is currently enrolled as a student in _____

Signed _____

Position _____

Southern cultures

For fastest service, please call [919] 962-4201,
Monday–Friday between 8:00 a.m. and 3:00 p.m. EST
with credit card information or fax your order to
[800] 272-6817. You can also send e-mail to
uncpress_journals@unc.edu.

INDIVIDUAL subscription request

Please enter my subscription to *Southern Cultures* at the rate of $39 for four quarterly issues. [Add $20 for postage outside the US.] *This price is good until December 31, 2011.*

☐ My check or money order, payable to THE UNIVERSITY OF NORTH
CAROLINA PRESS, is enclosed in an envelope with this card.

☐ Please charge my Visa or MasterCard [circle one].

CARD NUMBER _____ EXP. DATE _____

SIGNATURE _____ DAYTIME PHONE _____

NAME _____

ADDRESS _____ ZIP CODE _____

Southern cultures

For fastest service, please call [919] 962-4201,
Monday–Friday between 8:00 a.m. and 3:00 p.m. EST
with credit card information or fax your order to
[800] 272-6817. You can also send e-mail to
uncpress_journals@unc.edu.

INSTITUTION subscription request

Please enter my subscription to *Southern Cultures* at the rate of $57 for four quarterly issues. [Add $20 for postage outside the US.] *This price is good until December 31, 2011.*

☐ My check or money order, payable to THE UNIVERSITY OF NORTH
CAROLINA PRESS, is enclosed in an envelope with this card.

☐ Please charge my Visa or MasterCard [circle one].

CARD NUMBER _____ EXP. DATE _____

SIGNATURE _____ DAYTIME PHONE _____

NAME _____

ADDRESS _____ ZIP CODE _____